Letters on Vipassanā

Nina van Gorkom

November 2018

2

Published in 2018 by:
Zolag
32 Woodnook Road
Streatham
London
SW16 6TZ
www.zolag.co.uk

ISBN 9781897633342

British Library Cataloguing in Publication Data
A CIP record for this book is available from the British Library
Printed in the UK and USA by Lightningsource.

Contents

Preface

This book consists of a compilation of letters on the Dhamma to Sarah Abbott, Alan Weller, Robert Kirkpatrick and other friends. These letters were written in the period between 1980 until 1992. The material I have used are tapes of Acharn Sujin's lectures and conversations with her on the development of right understanding. She encourages people to develop understanding of the present moment, since that is the way to the ultimate goal, namely, the eradication of the clinging to the concept of self and of all other defilements. What the Buddha taught is not mere theory, but it is to be realized right now, at this moment. The Buddha taught that all mental phenomena and physical phenomena which naturally appear in our daily life can be object of mindfulness and right understanding.

I greatly appreciate Acharn Sujin's constant reminders to develop right understanding naturally, and not to force oneself to particular practices. Before one realizes it, one is lured by clinging to the idea of self. The scriptures are subtle, profound in meaning, and when one is reading them one may be deluded by wrong understanding. Acharn Sujin's clear explanations of the Dhamma are of immense value and can have a great impact on one's life. I hope that the reader will find these letters on vipassanā beneficial.

Introduction

I shall explain some terms and notions of the Dhamma I am using in order to facilitate the reading of this book.

It is essential to know the difference between what is real in conventional sense and what is real in the absolute or ultimate sense. If we only know conventional truth and do not know ultimate truth, the clinging to the concept of self and all other defilements cannot be eradicated. Notions such as person, world or tree are conventional truth, they are concepts we can think of, but they are not real in the ultimate sense. Mental phenomena or nāma and physical phenomena or rūpa are ultimate realities or paramattha dhammas. They have each their own inalterable characteristic, they are real for everybody; the names of realities can be changed but their characteristics are inalterable. Nāma is the reality which experiences something, whereas rūpa does not experience anything. Seeing, for example, is nāma, it experiences visible object which is rūpa. We may change the names "seeing" or "visible object", but their characteristics cannot be changed. Seeing is real for everybody, anger is real for everybody, no matter how we name it. A person is not real in the ultimate sense; what we take for a person are ever changing nāmas and rūpas.

Citta, or a moment of consciousness, is nāma, it experiences an object. Seeing is a citta which experiences visible object, hearing is a citta which experiences sound. Cittas experience their appropriate objects through six doors, the doors of the senses and the mind-door.

Cittas are variegated: some cittas are wholesome, kusala, some are unwholesome, akusala, and some are neither kusala nor akusala. One citta arises at a time and then falls away, to be succeeded by the next citta. Our life is an unbroken series of citta. Each citta is accompanied by several mental factors, cetasikas, which each perform their own function while they assist the citta in knowing the object. Some cetasikas accompany each citta, whereas other types of cetasikas accompany only particular types of citta. Attachment, lobha, aversion, dosa and ignorance, moha, are akusala cetasikas which accompany only akusala cittas. Non-attachment, alobha, non-aversion or kindness, adosa, and wisdom, amoha or paññā, are sobhana cetasikas, beautiful cetasikas, which can accompany only sobhana cittas.

Citta and cetasika which are both nāma, arise because of their appropriate conditions. Wholesome qualities and unwholesome qualities which arose in the past can condition the arising of such qualities at present. Since each citta is succeeded by the next one wholesome qualities and unwholesome qualities can be accumulated from one moment to the next moment, and thus there are conditions for their arising at the present time.

Some cittas are results of akusala kamma and kusala kamma, they are vipākacittas. Kamma is intention or volition. An unwholesome volition can motivate an unwholesome deed which can bring an unpleasant result later on, and a wholesome volition can motivate a wholesome deed which can bring a pleasant result later on. Akusala kamma and kusala kamma are accumulated from one moment to the next moment of citta, and thus they can produce result later on. Kamma produces result in the form of rebirth-consciousness, or, in the course of life, in the form of seeing, hearing, smelling, tasting and the experience of tangible object through the bodysense. These vipākacittas experience pleasant objects or unpleasant objects, depending on the kamma which produces them. Cittas which experience objects through the six doors arise in a process of cittas. When, for example, hearing arises, it occurs within a series or process of cittas, all of which experience sound. Only hearing-consciousness hears, but the other cittas within that process, which is called the ear-door process, perform each their own function. Hearing-consciousness is vipākacitta, it merely hears the sound, it neither likes it nor dislikes it. After hearing-consciousness has fallen away there are, within that process, akusala cittas or kusala cittas which experience the sound with unwholesomeness or with wholesomeness. There can be akusala cittas with attachment or with aversion towards the sound, or there can be kusala cittas. There are processes of cittas experiencing an object through the eye-door, the ear-door, the nose-door, the tongue-door, the body-door and the mind-door. After the cittas of a sense-door process have fallen away, the object is experienced by cittas arising in a mind-door process, and after that process has been completed there can be other mind-door processes of cittas which think of concepts. Cittas arise and fall away in succession so rapidly that it seems that cittas such as seeing and thinking of what is seen occur at the same time, but in reality there are different types of citta arising in different processes. We believe, for example, that we see a table, but in reality there is a process of cittas experiencing visible object through the eyesense, and then there is a process of cittas experiencing visible object through the mind-door, and later on there are other mind-door processes of cittas which think of the concept of table. For the development of right understanding it is important to know that there are different cittas which experience different objects through the six doorways.

Rūpa does not know or experience anything. What we call the body are different kinds of rūpa which arise and then fall away. Rūpas arise and fall away in groups or units of rūpas. Each group consists of several kinds of rūpas which always include four kinds of rūpas which are called the four Great Elements: the Element of Earth or solidity, appearing as hardness or softness, the Element of Water or cohesion, the Element of Fire or temperature, appearing as heat or cold, and the Element of Wind, appearing as motion or pressure. Solidity, temperature and motion or pressure are objects which can be experienced through the bodysense, whereas cohesion can only be experienced through the mind-door.

Intellectual understanding (pariyatti) can condition direct understanding of realities (paṭipatti) and this can condition the direct realization of the truth, paṭivedha. Pariyatti is not theoretical understanding, it is understanding of what appears now. When pariyatti has become very firm it can condition direct understanding, satipaṭṭhāna. Sati and paññā of the level of satipaṭṭhana are direct awareness and direct understanding of the nāma and rūpa appearing at the present moment.

There are many levels of sati; sati is heedful, non-forgetful, of what is wholesome. There is sati with generosity, dāna, with the observance of moral conduct, sīla, with the development of tranquil meditation, samatha, and with the development of right understanding of the present reality. Ultimate realities, nāma and rūpa, not concepts, are the objects of mindfulness and right understanding.

Understanding of mental phenomena and physical phenomena develops progressively in different stages. We come across the terms "development of the eightfold Path", "development of insight", vipassanā, and "development of satipaṭṭhāna" or the four Applications of Mindfulness. All these terms refer to the development of right understanding of mental phenomena, nāma, and physical phenomena, rūpa. By the teaching of the four Applications of Mindfulness the Buddha showed that all nāmas and rūpas which naturally appear in our daily life can be the objects of mindfulness and right understanding.

Letter 1

The object of mindfulness

Dear Dhamma friends,

Sarah and Jonothan traveled from Hong Kong to Bangkok in order have conversations with Acharn Sujin about the development of right understanding. I received the cassette tapes of these discussions and I would like to share with you what I learnt from these recordings.

The discussions dealt with the aim of the development of right understanding of realities which appear through the six doors. Acharn Sujin explained that it is useless to have many moments of sati of the level of satipaṭṭhāna without understanding anything, without understanding the reality which appears through one of the six doors. We should remember what the object of direct understanding and awareness is: paramattha dhammas, absolute realities, that is, nāma, mental phenomena, and rūpa, physical phenomena, appearing one at a time. Before we studied the Dhamma we knew only conventional truth, such as people, houses and trees. Through the Buddha's teachings we learn to know paramattha dhammas, nāma and rūpa. Citta, consciousness, is nāma, it experiences something. Rūpa is the reality which does not experience anything. Seeing is a citta, it experiences an object, visible object. Visible object is rūpa, it does not experience anything. It is useful to combine the study of the suttas with the study of the Abhidhamma, Acharn Sujin remarked, because this helps us to understand our life as different realities, as nāma and rūpa.

We should reflect more on the nature of citta, the reality which experiences an object. When we know more about the conditions for its arising we shall have more understanding of its characteristic of anattā, not self. Acharn Sujin said that different objects appear because cittas arise in processes which experience objects through the doors of eyes, ears, nose, tongue, bodysense or mind. When we are fast asleep there are no objects appearing through the different doorways. Bhavanga-cittas (life-continuum) arise and fall away in succession, and they have as their function to preserve the continuity of life as this particular person.[1] If there were no citta we would not be alive. When we are fast asleep we do not know any object of this world, we do not know who our parents are, what our possessions are, we are not involved with anything of this world. When we wake up we experience again the objects of this world. Visible object impinges on the eye-door and is experienced by seeing and by the other cittas of the eye-door process.[2] Sound impinges on the ear-door and the other sense objects impinge on their corresponding doorways. On account of the objects which are experienced there are mostly akusala cittas with like or dislike. We keep on thinking of the objects which are experienced through the senses and we create long stories about people and things. We take it for granted that different objects appear all day long, but, we should remember that they appear just because there are cittas arising in processes, in Pali:vīthi-cittas. In the case of seeing, several conditions are needed for seeing to experience

---

[1]Bhavanga-cittas do not experience objects through the six doors; they experience the same object as the rebirth-consciousness.

[2]See Intro.

visible object. Seeing is vipākacitta, the result of kamma, a deed performed in the past. Eyesense is also a condition for seeing; eyesense is produced by kamma. Visible object is another condition for seeing; if it would not impinge on the eyesense there could not be seeing. Seeing sees visible object, and after seeing has fallen away we pay attention to shape and form which is not seeing. It is important to reflect on the difference between seeing and thinking of concepts such as people and things. In that way, it will be clearer that realities such as seeing and visible object can be the objects of mindfulness and right understanding, and that conventional truth, concepts or ideas, are objects of thinking but not objects of right understanding. However, the reality which thinks about concepts is a type of nāma and thus it can be object of understanding. When there is more intellectual understanding of the reality appearing at the present moment and this has become firm, there can be the right conditions for the arising of direct awareness and understanding of the characteristics of realities.

I shall quote from a letter of Alan Weller in England, who describes his own experience concerning the study of Dhamma, in order to encourage my husband Lodewijk:

"I remember getting stuck with Acharn Sujin's tapes, listening to the same ones over and over again. Books like the Visuddhimagga used to send me to sleep. I could not cope with the endless classifications. However, very gradually I just keep on walking. I have no problems now with the Visuddhimagga and I delight in its precision. The teachings are so wide, books, recordings, discussions with people. I like to study what I am interested in and if I find something tiring or difficult I turn to what I find interesting. The Jātaka stories are very easy to read and so useful for daily life. The wide reading is a condition to have great respect for Acharn Sujin's words, for without those recordings I could not understand the depth of the Dhamma or have the confidence that I have now. This is my advice to

Lodewijk: just keep on walking."

Alan refers to what Acharn Sujin once said in India: "Keep on walking, even if it is just one step at a time." We should have more confidence in the value of listening to the Dhamma, studying the scriptures and considering the reality appearing now. We can be sure that in this way there will be conditions for the arising of direct awareness and direct understanding later on, which is different from thinking about realities.

The gradual development of understanding is in the scriptures (Gradual Sayings, Book of the Sevens, Ch VII, § 7) compared to the wearing out of a knife handle which one holds each day. However, it wears out so slowly that one cannot see its wearing away. A friend remarked that if one's practice is right one should see some progress. He found that there was no sati while working in his office. The world of work seems to be different from the world of Dhamma. He thought that being under stress was not a good condition for sati. One should be in the right mood and have some leisure time.

Acharn Sujin answered that this is only thinking. One should know the difference between a moment of understanding a reality and thinking. Only through satipaṭṭhāna one can know the difference. This is a good reminder. We are so involved in our thoughts about having understanding, in finding ways to have more, but what is there right at that moment? Only a nāma which thinks. When we realize this, the infatuation is gone, no more worry. Acharn Sujin said:

"Do not think of the past or the future. Realities appear, why do you have to move away from them. That is not the way to understand this moment. There is seeing, hearing, smelling, tasting, touching or thinking, no matter whether one is working or not."

If one does not know that there are cittas which experience objects through the six doors one cannot develop understanding of this moment. Time and again objects such as visible object, sound or tangible object are appearing. They can only appear because there is citta which experiences them. Did we consider this enough? There may be sound but if hearing-consciousness does not arise sound is not an object which is experienced, sound does not appear. We believe that we see the world of people and different things, but there is only citta which thinks about what has appeared to seeing. Seeing does not occur at the same time as thinking. Seeing experiences visible object which has impinged on the eyesense, it does not pay attention to shape and form. However, seeing conditions thinking of shape and form, of defining them as people and different things. Acharn Sujin writes in her book "A Survey of Paramattha Dhammas":

"Since cittas succeed one another very rapidly, it seems that there is the world which does not disintegrate, the world which is lasting and which is full of beings and many different things. In reality the world lasts just for one moment and then it falls away."

If we have a bowl of fruits on the table we can look at them and they do not seem to fall away. It is helpful to know the reason. Realities, paramattha dhammas, such as visible object which is a kind of rūpa, fall away. However, we keep on thinking about the stories we create. The concepts such as fruit we can think of are not paramattha dhammas, they are not realities; thus, they do not arise and fall away. They are merely made up by our thinking. Acharn Sujin said:

"When one is busy with one's work, when there is non-forgetfulness, one can begin to have some understanding, even though it be very little, of what is real. Citta is real, it experiences an object. A dead body, even if there are still eyes and ears, cannot experience anything. Citta experiences. The experience is a reality. We should not be attached to the idea of, 'how can I have more sati'. It can grow in a few lifetimes. Let us talk about seeing and visible object. If there is no understanding of this moment how can understanding grow? Considering visible object in the office is not different from considering visible object at this moment. There is no need to change the situation or to do anything else in order to develop right understanding."

We read in the "Gradual Sayings" (Book of the Fours, First Fifty, Ch I, § 6) about four kinds of people: a person of small learning who doesn't profit thereby, a person of small learning who profits thereby, a person of wide learning who doesn't profit thereby and a person of wide learning who profits thereby. We read:

> In this case, monks, a certain person has small learning in Sutta, Geyya, Veyyākaraa, Gāthā, Udāna, Itivuttaka, Jātaka, Abbhutadhammā and Vedalla[3]; yet, as of that small learning he knows not the letter, knows not the meaning, he does not live in accordance with Dhamma. That, monks, is how a person with small learning profits not thereby.
>
> And in what way, monks, is a person of small learning profited thereby? In this case, monks, a certain person has small learning in Sutta...; but, as of that small learning he knows both the letter and the meaning, he lives in accordance with Dhamma. That, monks, is how a person of small learning profits thereby.

We then read about the person with wide learning who does not profit thereby and the person of wide learning who profits thereby. Of these two kinds of persons the same is said as in the case of the person with small learning who does not profit thereby and the person with small learning who profits thereby.

According to the commentary, the "Manorathapūraī" the person with small learning who lives in accordance with the

---

[3]A classification of the Dhamma as suttas without and with verses, expository matter including Abhidhamma, Birth stories, marvels, etc.

Dhamma, who profits thereby, has eradicated the āsavas[4]. The same is true for the person with wide learning who profits thereby.

Alan Weller wrote:

"The last few weeks I have been very busy and have had little time for reading or writing. The sutta about profiting even from small learning is very useful. I often find myself wanting to read or study and I am forgetful of the reality which is there at that moment. We all need lots of details because defilements are so crafty to move us away from the present moment."

People may have misunderstandings about the development of understanding of realities, they doubt whether it can be developed also during the time they are working. These misunderstandings arise because they believe that they should concentrate on realities in order to have right understading of them. We should know that there can be wrong concentration, arising with akusala citta. Concentration is a cetasika, a mental factor[5], which arises with each citta. Its function is to focus on one object at a time. Concentration does not last, it falls away immediately together with the citta it accompanies. If one thinks that one has to concentrate on nāma and rūpa there is thinking with attachment. One tries to control sati but that is impossible. When there are conditions for the arising of right mindfulness and right understanding, there is also right concentration without the need to think of concentration.

Citta and cetasika are conditioned nāmas. There is one citta at a time and each citta is accompanied by several cetasikas which each perform their own function while they assist the citta in knowing an object. If we do not know that understanding, mindfulness and right concentration are cetasikas which accompany kusala citta, we shall cling to them and have wrong view about them. We need to know many details because defilements are deeply rooted.

---

[4]The "Intoxicants", a group of defilements.
[5]See Intro.

If one develops understanding naturally one does not try to exert control over understanding or over its objects. A moment of right understanding may arise and after that moments of forgetfulness. One can learn to notice the difference between such moments. Does at this moment a paramattha dhamma appear, or does one think of a concept?

Jonothan remarked that visible object is different from what we think it is. We tend to speculate about it, but in reality it is just that which is seen. All that appears through the eyesense is visible object. If one were blind it could not appear. Acharn Sujin asked whether visible object can move. When we notice a change of position of what we perceive it is only thinking. Because of remembrance of past experiences one believes that one sees people move. If there can be a moment of awareness of one reality there will be less clinging to a concept of a "whole" to an image of a person walking.

When we hear a dog barking, different moments of experience arise. Hearing hears that particular sound and then we remember that it is the sound of a dog. We can remind ourselves that it is not "I"who remembers but saññā, remembrance or perception, a cetasika which remembers an object or "marks"it so that it can be recognized later on. Saññā accompanies each citta, be it seeing or hearing or the citta which thinks of concepts. We recognize people and things because of saññā. Previous experiences are remembered because of saññā. Also in the past the sound of a dog was heard, we learnt what a dog is and the way it barks. Because of saññā we can imitate its barking, or, when other people imitate its barking we can know that it is not the barking of a dog. "Sound does not know that you are thinking about it" Acharn Sujin said, reminding us that there is no being, no dog in the sound. It is only rūpa which impinges on the earsense; when there are the right conditions a particular sound, pleasant or unpleasant, can be heard. The sound only appears when it is the right time for vīthi-cittas[6] arising in the ear-door process. When we are fast asleep there may be sound, but it is not heard.

Seeing, hearing and the other sense-cognitions are followed by thinking which thinks about what was experienced. We are absorbed in the concepts we are thinking of. Acharn Sujin said that it takes time to realize that one lives with one's own thoughts, in one's own world of thinking. It is useful to know about the function of the cetasika vitakka, which can be translated as thinking. It accompanies many cittas, though not every citta. It "touches" the object which is experienced, or it leads citta to the object, so that citta can experience it. We read in the suttas about vitakka which is akusala: thinking with desire, with hatred and with cruelty. We also read about vitakka which is sobhana (beautiful): thinking with detachment (nekkhamma), with non-aversion or kindness, and with non-violence. There is right thinking, sammā-sankappa, of the eightfold Path. It "touches" the object of awareness, a nāma or a rūpa, so that paññā can know it as it is.

If we do not know that thinking is due to the activity of vitakka we are bound to take it for self. We think most of the time with akusala citta, we can become confused by the stories we create ourselves.

Someone wrote to me that he was infatuated with his own fantasies which went on for a long time. He found himself a mean person because of that. If one thinks of oneself as a mean person one takes one's akusala for "self" One can learn from such experiences that thinking is beyond control, anattā. Defilements arise because there are conditions for their arising. The writer of the letter thought that his fantasies were the consequence of the education he had had. However, this is merely a "story" one may think of but which does not explain the deepest cause. It can happen to all of us that we suddenly, for no ap-

---

[6] Cittas arising in a process, see Intro.

parent reason, have very ugly thoughts, thoughts of jealousy or even thoughts of hatred, and we may wonder where these come from. There were countless lives before this life, and during these lives we accumulated many defilements. We do not know what our past lives were like, but during the cycle there must have been unhappy rebirths, such as birth as an animal. The defilements of all past lives have been accumulated from moment to moment and they can arise at any time with akusala citta, they can even motivate bad deeds. We experience sense objects usually with akusala cittas becaus we accumulated such an amount of akusala. When we notice our defilements it is of no use to keep on thinking about them with aversion; then we will only accumulate more akusala. We can learn to develop right understanding also of akusala which arises, in order to see it as not self, only a conditioned reality. Acharn Sujin explained:

"We should be brave and encounter the reality at that very moment with right understanding, then there is right effort. It is difficult to follow the Middle Way, that is, to follow all realities naturally. Through right understanding one will see more clearly one's own akusala, also the more subtle attachment to sense objects."

The study of the Abhidhamma can remind us that the different cittas which are accompanied by cetasikas arise because of their own conditions and fall away immediately. When one, for example, has the intention to abstain from akusala but one cannot do so in a particular situation, one should remember that it is not self who can abstain but that there are cetasikas, "virati[7] cetasikas" which have the function of abstaining. They are: abstention from wrong speech, from wrong action and from wrong livelihood. When virati cetasika does not arise we cannot possibly abstain from akusala. The development of right understanding of whatever reality appears now can condition abstention from akusala.

---

[7]Virati means abstinence.

We read in the "Stories of the Mansions"(Khuddaka Nikāya, Vimānavatthu, V, Great Chariot, 53, the Mansion of Chatta) that the brahman youth Chatta was on his way to pay his teacher. Thieves were waiting for him in order to kill and rob him. The Buddha sat under a tree on the road Chatta was taking and he taught him out of compassion the three refuges and the five precepts. Chatta continued on his way, reflecting on the Buddha's teaching, and then he was killed by the robbers. He was reborn a deva and showed himself with his luminous mansion. The Buddha asked him of which deed his rebirth was the result so that many people would know the deed of merit Chatta had done. Chatta explained that he first did not want to take the three refuges and that he afterwards did so. Evenso he did not want to take the five precepts but afterwards he did so. We read that he said:

> I approached the glorious Conquerer for refuge, and
> Dhamma too, likewise the Order of monks. First
> I said "No" revered sir; afterwards I did your bid-
> ding faithfully. Live not in any way impurely, hurt-
> ing any breathing thing, for wise men do not praise
> lack of restraint towards breathing things. First I
> said "No" revered sir; afterwards I did your bidding
> faithfully...

We read that, after the teaching of each of the five precepts, he first said "No" and then afterwards, took the precept. We read further on:

> Even a little done in the Tathāgata's Dhamma is
> of great fruition, a wide-spread fruit. Behold how
> Chatta, through merit done, illumines the earth even
> as does the sun ...

It can happen to all of us that we first say "No" when we think that we cannot abstain from akusala. When we learn that understanding of realities should be developed naturally, in daily life, also in the situation of our work, we may at first say, "No, I cannot do it." But when there are conditions for kusala citta with right understanding we see that it can be done. However, we should remember that it cannot be done by a "self". We may think, "No, I cannot be aware of akusala, I must make it disappear first." When there is more understanding of citta and cetasika which arise because of their own conditions we can learn that whatever arises cannot be changed, but that understanding of it can be developed.

Someone was wondering why it is necessary to learn so many details about citta, cetasika and rūpa. Is it not enough to read just one page of the scriptures one's whole life? Acharn Sujin answered that the Buddha did not have to teach for a long time to those who had conditions to attain enlightenment soon. However, for us it is different. We may read, "Seeing is impermanent" but this is not enough for us. We need to listen much, read and study much and consider the present reality often. We have to learn to develop right understanding of the characteristics of the realities which appear now. Kusala citta and akusala citta can arise shortly one after the other and there has to be more understanding so that their different characteristics can be known. Kusala citta with pleasant feeling may arise and after that akusala citta with pleasant feeling and attachment to the idea of "my kusala" may arise. Do we know the difference between such moments?

A friend said that she likes to earn money with her work since that gives her an opportunity to travel to Bangkok or to her home country. But she finds that the Dhamma makes one feel ashamed of liking to earn money. Acharn Sujin said: "You don't understand yourself completely, you are not honest with yourself. One should understand one's own accumulations."

Those who have attained enlightenment are "people who walk straight" (in Pali: "ujupatipanno". They know their accumulations, they are honest to themselves. Sometimes I feel ashamed about liking to read magazines and novels. However, understanding should be developed naturally, so that one realizes one's accumulated inclinations as not self. Next to my bed I have suttas as well as magazines and novels. At times I take up a sutta, at times a magazine or novel. I cannot tell beforehand what I will do, it is dependent on conditions. Also while reading a magazine there can be a few moments of considering visible object and then one is absorbed again in the story, which is a different moment.

When we look at other people understanding of realities can be developed naturally. When we see colours of hair, lips, eyebrows or skin, we think of them as belonging to the body, but we should remember that all these colours are just visible object, they appear through the eyesense. They could not appear if we close our eyes. Colour which appears is not the same colour all over, it is not all grey or black. Many different colours appear but they are just visible object, they are experienced by seeing.

There is such a great variety of colours, sounds, odours, flavours and tangible objects which appear and are experienced by the appropriate sense-cognitions through the corresponding sense-doors. After the sense-door process has been completed, the object is experienced through the mind-door, and then there are other mind-door processes of cittas which define the object and think about it.

Acharn Sujin reminds us time and again that we should always be humble, a "nobody" instead of somebody. A wise person who understands realities which arise because of their own conditions will be less attracted by honour, praise or gain. Do we think of "my development" is there an idea of "I did it" Then we want to be somebody, and that is not the right way.

A friend remarked that it is very hard to see the danger and disadvantage of the impermanence of nāma and rūpa, of their arising and falling away. Acharn Sujin answered:

"Even when the arising and falling away of realities is experienced it is not enough. Attachment and the other defilements are so deeply rooted. It needs higher and higher understanding to see the danger of the arising and falling away of nāma and rūpa. They appear and then disappear immediately, but the succeeding ones arise and thus there will be attachment again. Attachment is so attached to any object which arises. We can talk a great deal about the impermanence of realities, but this does not mean anything if the reality of this moment is not directly experienced as impermanent."

The friend asked:

"Is it of any use at all to think of the impermanence of realities if it is not directly experienced?"

Acharn Sujin answered:

"It is right thinking which is wholesome, but it cannot eradicate akusala. That is why the Buddha told us to develop more understanding. One may read the scriptures but if there is no understanding of the present moment we shall remain ignorant of what has been taught in the scriptures."

Letter 2

The Middle Way

When Acharn Sujin was in England Alan Weller recorded the discussions he had with her. These recordings contain many precious reminders about understanding of realities in daily life and, therefore, I would like to share these. The discussions were about citta (consciousness), cetasika (mental factors arising with the citta) and rūpa (physical phenomena). They were about cittas which experience objects through the six doors of eyes, ears, nose, tongue, bodysense and mind.

Many different types of citta arise in daily life. There is seeing of visible object and there is the interpretation of what was seen and this is not seeing but thinking. When there are conditions for understanding it can arise and know any object which appears, be it visible object, seeing, feeling or thinking. We do not have to name or label any reality. Seeing is just the experience of what is visible, it has its own characteristic, we do not have to name it. Thinking is just thinking, it has its own characteristic, we do not have to name it.

Seeing sees visible object, but it lasts only for an extremely short moment and then it is gone. Visible object does not last either, it falls away. Seeing can only see, it cannot think of

15

visible object. If one wants to concentrate on seeing or visible object, if one has any idea of fixing one's attention on them with the purpose of knowing them, it prevents right understanding of realities. We cannot stare at visible object, since it is seen just for a moment, and then it falls away. We may think about it, but that is not understanding of its characteristic. I would like to transcribe a dialogue between Acharn Sujin and Alan about this subject:

Acharn Sujin: "The more one understands that thinking thinks, the more visible object will appear as visible object. It does not matter at all if thinking arises; there are conditions for thinking almost all the time. There is the experience of objects through the sense-doors and then thinking."

Alan: "We have to know, not through thinking, but through direct experience."

Acharn: "That is why there should be understanding of thinking as just a reality. Many people do not want to think, they try to stop thinking. They believe that in that way they can understand realities."

Alan: "The thinking is very fast. Seeing sees visible object and then thinking arises." Acharn: "Visible object appears very shortly and then there is thinking. One thinks about a particular thing."

Alan: "We are picking out one thing from the visible object by our thinking. Just one idea."

Acharn: "Then some 'thing' is there, even if we do not name it. When we point at something there is thinking, not seeing. For the experience of visible object you don't have to point."

Alan: "I was looking at curtains but I did not notice the pattern of pine-apples, because I was not thinking of it. Only when someone said that there were pine-apples I recognized the pine-apples."

Acharn: "Because then you were thinking about it. What is seen now is just a reality and then the thinking thinks a lot. This happens all the time, no matter whether you read a book, watch T.V., look at paintings or look while you walk in the street. Understanding can come to know the true nature of realities at such moments."

Alan: "There are just different types of thinking when one selects things from the visible object. "

Acharn: "One begins to understand that there is nobody, thinking thinks only."

Alan: "Thinking is just a reality which thinks. There is no one, just realities. That is the meaning of being alone."

Acharn: "This is the way to become detached from realities we used to take for 'I'. There is all the time the idea of 'I think', 'I see'; 'I,I,I', all the time. There is not only visible object, there is also sound. There is sound which appears, then visible object, then sound again, all such moments are extremely short."

Alan: "When we pay attention to shape and form is there usually lobha (attachment)?"

Acharn: "When the feeling is not unpleasant, thus, pleasant or indifferent, there is usually lobha. Lobha arises when we read a newspaper or look at a picture, but realities of daily life can be understood."

Alan: "I think that there is no difference between this or that particular situation."

Acharn: "There is no difference at all. The six doorways are the same, everywhere. No matter one moves around or looks at something, right understanding of realities can arise. We may think about other people and wonder why they behave like that, but what about our own citta?"

We may have aversion about someone else's behaviour, but aversion falls away and instead of thinking for a long time about it there can be understanding of whatever reality appears.

Some people, when they hear about citta, cetasika and rūpa, say that they do not like the Abhidhamma, that they prefer the suttas. They think that the Abhidhamma is too theoreti-

cal. It depends on one's personal inclination to what extent one
will study the Abhidhamma, but if there is no knowledge at all
about nāma, the reality which experiences something, and rūpa,
the reality which does not experience anything, one cannot develop the eightfold path. One does not know what the object
of understanding is. One does not know that a concept such as
the whole body or a person cannot be object of understanding;
it is only an object of thinking. One nāma or rūpa at a time
as it appears through one of the six doors can be the object of
understanding. If one begins to understand the characteristic of
seeing which appears, or the characteristic of visible object, or
the characteristic of any other reality which appears, one will
know that the Abhidhamma explains the realities of our daily
life. Also the suttas are full of Abhidhamma, one cannot really
understand them without any knowledge of paramattha dhammas. Time and again we read in the suttas about the objects
which are experienced through the six doors, we read about seeing, hearing, smelling, tasting, the experience of tangible object
and the experience of objects through the mind-door. If we do
not know that the experiences of the objects through the six
doorways are different cittas, we take all experiences for self.

We learn through the Abhidhamma and also through the
suttas that cittas are accompanied by different cetasikas, mental
factors. Not everybody is inclined to study cetasikas in detail,
but if one does not know anything about them one does not
see that akusala citta is different from kusala citta because they
are accompanied by different types of cetasikas. Defilements as
well as wholesome qualities are cetasikas which accompany citta.
The factors of the eightfold Path, such as right understanding
and right mindfulness, are cetasikas. When these factors which
accompany kusala citta arise, the eightfold Path is being developed, just for a moment, and then citta and the accompanying
cetasikas fall away. Sati and paññā can be accumulated and
then there are conditions for another moment of developing the

eightfold Path, later on. Understanding develops from moment to moment. If we understand that life exists only in one moment, we shall be less inclined to believe that there is a self who could develop the eightfold Path continuously. This would not be according to the truth, because the next moment is likely to be akusala. If we know that right effort is a cetasika which arises just for a moment we shall cling less to an idea of self who exerts effort in the development of the eightfold Path.

We think that we should develop understanding, but actually it is understanding, paññā, which develops. There is nobody who develops understanding. Acharn Sujin remarked:

"In the beginning it seems that 'I' am developing, but later on one realizes that it is right understanding, paññā, which grows. One comes to the conclusion that nobody can do anything."

Alan said:

"Because each moment is conditioned, one can't do anything or control anything, not even the development of right understanding. It is conditioned by what one has learnt or considered."

Acharn Sujin remarked:

"Even if one considers oneself a Buddhist, it depends on conditions whether one can read wisely or consider wisely. Or does one just want to be 'somebody' instead of developing right understanding?

It is quite difficult to develop understanding of visible object at this moment, to realize that there is not anybody in the visible object which is seen. It takes time to listen again and again, to consider realities again and again. Without understanding of this moment there is no way to eliminate desire. There is desire if one wants to have a special experience instead of developing understanding. I do not tell anybody to do this or that first in order to develop understanding, there is no technique which should be applied. One thinks too much and tries too much. When can there be satipaṭṭhāna? When there is enough understanding to condition it."

Direct understanding cannot occur if pariyatti, intellectual
understanding of what appears now, has not been developed
sufficiently. One wishes for satipaṭṭhāna, for stages of insight,
vipassanā, but if there is such a wish, is there not an idea of self?
We should not force ourselves to reach something for which we
are not ready yet. Acharn Sujin said:

"This moment of gaining understanding is enough for this
moment, and, thus, the development can continue naturally.
There should be contentedness with one's own ability.

We should be grateful to the Buddha for the understanding
we have gained already, even if it is not a great deal yet. If there
is not much understanding now, it is because it was not developed much in the past. It takes aeons to develop it. We should
remember that right understanding is a conditioned reality, we
cannot hasten its development. If we try to do so, we are clinging to the idea of self. However, understanding is developed in
order to get rid of the idea of self."

A friend wrote to me about a meditation technique he applies
in order to experience the impermanence of rūpas of the body.
Through concentration on rūpas of the body he thinks that he
can experience the change of rūpas such as heat of the body.
He finds it such an intellectual struggle to grasp the truth of
anattā (non-self) and through the experience of impermanence
he believes that he can realize the truth of anattā more easily.
He thinks that by this method all the stages of insight, vipassanā
ñāṇas, can be reached.

When the rūpa which is heat appears, there must also be
nāma which experiences heat. In order to know the truth there
should not only be understanding of rūpa but also of nāma,
the element which experiences something. If there is no right
understanding which realizes nāma as nāma and rūpa as rūpa,
there is an idea of self who feels hot or "my body" which is hot.
There is "somebody" or "something" there, thus, one clings to

a "self". There is the deeply rooted idea of self, even when we do not think, "I feel", or "This is my body".

It is not easy to understand the meaning of anattā, as the writer of the letter remarks. We should consider what the Buddha taught about anattā . He clearly showed the conditions for each reality which arises. Since there are conditions for the nāmas and rūpas which arise we cannot exert control over their arising. "Beyond control" is one way to describe the nature of anattā. When the right conditions are present, a rūpa such as heat may impinge on the bodysense. Bodysense is a kind of rūpa which is produced by kamma. Nobody can create his own bodysense. The bodysense is all over the body, it can be outside or inside. When heat impinges on the bodysense there are conditions for the arising of body-consciousness which experiences the heat just for a short moment and then it falls away. It merely experiences the heat and it does not know anything else.

Feeling accompanies the body-consciousness, it is a cetasika which feels on account of the tangible object which is experienced. When tangible object is pleasant, pleasant bodily feeling accompanies body-consciousness, and when it is unpleasant, painful bodily feeling accompanies body-consciousness. Shortly afterwards there are likely to be akusala cittas which may be akusala cittas rooted in attachment, accompanied by pleasant or by indifferent feeling, or akusala cittas rooted in aversion, accompanied by unpleasant feeling, or akusala cittas rooted in ignorance, accompanied by indifferent feeling. Sometimes there can be kusala cittas accompanied by pleasant feeling or by indifferent feeling. We can learn that when the feeling is not unpleasant there is usually attachment to objects.

At first it may seem easy to have understanding only of rūpas of the body. When we learn more about different types of nāma and rūpa we can see that it is not easy to have precise knowledge of any of them.

When heat appears its characteristic can be known as only

a rūpa. We do not have to think whether it is external heat or internal heat, we do not have to think of the spot of the body where it appears. It is only a rūpa which appears just for a moment, it does not belong to "my body", it is beyond control. Understanding of the different types of nāma and rūpa which appear through the appropriate doorways develops very gradually. It is only later on that paññā can realize the three general characteristics of nāma and rūpa, which are impermanence, dukkha (unsatistactoriness) and anattā.

When there are the right conditions kusala citta accompanied by sati and paññā can arise. One cannot select any object of understanding, all realities which appear are beyond control. The Buddha spoke about the six doors in order to remind people that all realities of daily life should be known as they are.

It is not easy at all to know precisely, through direct understanding, what nāma is and what rūpa. When paññā is still weak we are not sure whether a characteristic of rūpa or of nāma appears. Understanding has to be developed again and again. When hardness or heat are experienced, we may have doubts whether that was mindfulness and direct understanding or not. The fact that hardness or heat can be directly experienced without having to think about them does not mean that there is direct understanding of them. They are directly experienced by body-consciousness which is vipākacitta, and this citta is not accompanied by sati and paññnā. After that there may be akusala cittas with subtle clinging to hardness or heat, but one may take that for mindfulness. When one tries to concentrate on realities in order to know them there is akusala citta with clinging; there is desire to know, not mindfulness.

The following sutta can remind us that there should be the development of understanding of rūpa as rūpa and of nāma as nāma, as elements devoid of self. We read in the "Kindred Sayings" (II, Nidāna-vagga, Ch XIV, Elements, § 1) that the Buddha, while he was at Sāvatthī, said to the monks:

What, monks, is the diversity in elements? The elements of eye, of visible object, of seeing-consciousness; the elements of ear, of sound, of hearing-consciousness; the elements of nose, of odour, of smelling-consciousness; the elements of tongue, of taste, of tasting-consciousness; the elements of body-sense, of tangibles, of body-consciousness; the elements of mind, of mental objects, of the experience of mental objects. This, monks, is called diversity in elements.

Seeing can only arise when there are visible object and eye-sense, thus, it can only arise when there are the appropriate conditions. The nāma-elements and rūpa-elements of our life arise because of conditions, they are not self, they are beyond control. When heat appears, understanding of its characteristic can be developed for that short moment, so that it can be known as a rūpa element. It is rūpa, not part of "my body", not self. It does not know anything, it is different from nāma. When feeling appears, understanding can be developed of its characteristic as a nāma element. It is nāma, an element which experiences something, different from rūpa. There is no self who experiences.

The difference between nāma and rūpa cannot be clearly known before paññā of the level of intellectual understanding has been developed to direct understanding of realities. Insight, direct understanding, is developed in stages and at the first stage it clearly distinguishes nāma from rūpa. This level of understanding may seem to be far away, but it is useful to know that this is the first stage. Otherwise one may mistake thinking for direct understanding. When one experiences changes of the body temperature or notices the appearance and disappearance of sound, one may believe that one experiences the impermanence of rūpas. However, the arising and falling away of nāma and rūpa is the fourth stage of insight or the first stage of "principal insight", mahā-vipassanā, and this cannot be realized if the first stage of "tender insight" has not been reached.[1]

Life exists only in a moment. When we consider this more we shall be less inclined to cling to the concept of a thing or a person. When we cling to someone or dislike someone it is only thinking. We always think of people, but when understanding arises we know whether we think with kusala citta or with akusala citta, with loving kindness or with aversion. Acharn Sujin said:

"When we have aversion we should find out whether it is a name or a reality which is the object of aversion. A name represents a person. When you think of a name you think of someone. Right understanding can find out that it is thinking again. One lives with one's own thoughts. Develop loving kindness instead of having aversion towards what is only a name."

When we understand that a person, in the ultimate sense, exists only in our thoughts, we can appreciate the following reminder:

"What we consider as a friend in conventional terms is only an idea. When you have a friend what does it mean? About what do you talk? 'What shall we do tomorrow, where are we going, what shall we eat?' Thus it means that you associate with someone's opinion which you consider as a friend. These are moments of thinking. We may associate with wrong opinions or with right opinions and that influences our way of life."

Acharn Sujin also spoke to Alan about married life:

"We are attached to many things in life but we know that it is for a very short time. You can change your mind. One will be married or single according to one's accumulations. But don't forget the development of understanding. You should not think that your attachment to a person will last as long as you live. Every moment arises because of conditions. There can be a

---

[1] The first three stages of insight are beginning stages or "tender insight", taruṇa vipassanā. They precede the first stage of principal insight, which is followed by other stages, until enlightenment is attained. This will be further explained in Letter 6.

change in the relationship because of your own accumulations or because of the other person's accumulations. Attachment brings sorrow, no matter it lasts long or short. If one really studies one's cittas one can understand that there are many degrees of attachment. Sometimes one wants something so much for oneself, even if one likes the other person. You are attached to that person but you want something for yourself. If we study our life closely we just love ourselves. Everything is just for the sake of our own feeling, our own pleasure. Nothing is permanent. This helps us to see the true nature of reality. We can gain something from each moment, even when there is a loss. Even a loss does not bring me much pain, I get something from it. It is good if one is prepared, ready to face any unpleasant situation. The understanding of the Dhamma can help one in many situations about which one would otherwise feel unhappy."

Alan asked Acharn Sujin:

"Should one in daily life not be very careful so that one is not caught up with pleasant things, non-Dhamma things?"

Acharn Sujin answered:

"I think one cannot live without pleasure, and one cannot live without Dhamma. One cannot live with ignorance, having just pleasure. The wise person cannot live just for pleasure. He will live with pleasure and with understanding."

This is the Middle Way. If we are honest we know that we have accumulations for enjoyment, why deny it? But understanding can develop naturally of all realities which appear, also of pleasure. We do not have to wait or change conditions. The Middle Way is the right way, but it is difficult. Progress is bound to be slow and because of desire one may try to flee from daily life, try to exert effort and concentrate on realities. Acharn Sujin spoke again and again about the natural way of developing understanding. She said:

"When one enjoys something very much one cannot prevent it, but there can be right understanding. That is the eightfold

Path. One should understand all conditioned realities which occur in one's life. Seeing is conditioned, pleasant feeling and unpleasant feeling are conditioned. They have their own conditions already. We should not 'prepare' conditions for anything to arise. Nobody can condition any reality at all. When there is a very low level of understanding, begin again, begin again. When one has precise understanding of the Middle Way, one will not turn away. One can easily turn away because of lobha."

When one hears about about the natural way of developing understanding, even in the midst of enjoyment, one may wonder where the right effort of the eightfold Path comes in. It comes in exactly when we begin again, begin again. When we are not disheartened about our low level of understanding and there is courage for sati and paññā now, there is right effort accompanying right understanding, even though we are only in a beginning stage of developing the eightfold Path. We do not have to think of making an effort, then there would be an idea of self who exerts effort. There can be understanding of the flux of realities which is our life.

Letter 3

Anattā in daily life

Through the study of the Dhamma we learn that we are mis-led by the outer appearance of things. As soon as we open our eyes it seems that we see continuously. Even when thinking or hearing arises it seems that there can still be seeing at the same time. More than one experience at a time seems to occur, but in reality only one citta at a time arises, experiences an object through the appropriate doorway, and then falls away. We may believe that our body can feel pleasant and unpleasant things, but in reality, what we take for our body are only physical phe-nomena, rūpas, which cannot experience anything. The more we study the Dhamma the more we realize that we have accumu-lated wrong ideas about the phenomena in ourselves and around ourselves. Should we not find out more about the realities of our life?

We understand in theory that there is no self, but under-standing has not been developed to the stage that the truth of anattā, not self, can be directly realized. At this moment we are full of the idea of self and our clinging to the self is bound to hinder the development of right understanding. We cling to "our kusala" and we have aversion towards "our akusala"; we do not see these realities as they are, as not self. Are we not annoyed when there is disturbance of mind, forgetfulness and distraction in a day? Then we have aversion towards "our akusala". We wish to improve the situation and become calm, undisturbed and mindful, in order to accumulate a great deal of kusala, "our kusala". Instead of right understanding of realities which arise because of their own conditions, our goal becomes the accumulation of kusala. Then we are moving away from our real goal: detachment from the self through right understanding.

Alan Driver, a Dhamma friend who passed away, clearly understood that we can easily be moved away from our real goal. I shall quote from his words :

"So very often our aim is not really to understand whatever appears right now. We want to get rid of distraction, to be calmer, to be steadier, to be more organised, to be somehow other than we are. What is that if it is not attachment?

Why can't we just be aware of distraction? But, oh no, we don't like distraction and there we are, thoroughly distracted from awareness, because of our attachment to a self who does not want to be distracted. In fact, this is attachment to peace, not the development of understanding.

Ask yourself, do you really want to be aware or do you want calm? We just go on perpetuating the illusion of a self who has got a job to do and who wants to do it and does not like distraction which gets in the way of doing the job. That is not right understanding at all. It is a cause for more frustration when distraction arises. Only at a moment of right understanding is there any interest, right interest in the object that appears, in order to see it as it really is. We are always looking for some other object, trying to change it or make it last. That is attachment, not detachment."

If we are honest with ourselves we shall notice when we are diverted from the right Path in choosing another goal, such as the gaining of kusala for ourselves. I am grateful for being reminded of the true goal. There should be detachment from the very beginning. When heat appears it can be known as rūpa, a reality which does not experience anything. It is not part of "my body", it is not "mine". We never know what reality will appear next, a reality which is pleasant, unpleasant, kusala or akusala. If we try to direct understanding to this object first and then to that, for example to rūpas appearing in the body or to feelings, there is again an idea of self and we shall never know that understanding is anattā.

Someone wrote that a teacher in a meditation center told people to get rid of akusala as soon as possible. When it arises one should concentrate more deeply on particular realities such as feelings. He also said that one burns up old kamma by the accumulation of kusala cittas while one is practising vipassanā.

Akusala kamma is past already and we cannot prevent it from producing its result. The ariyan who has attained enlightenment has no more conditions for an unhappy rebirth, but he still receives unpleasant results through the senses in the course of his life. We cannot know which kamma produces which result at a particular moment, only a Buddha can know this. There were countless lives in the past with countless akusala kammas. Who can claim that he can accumulate a great deal of kusala and can burn up old kamma? When we are having such thoughts we are clinging to the accumulation of kusala, we are again off the right Path.

Akusala citta may arise and after it has fallen away paññā can realize it as a conditioned nāma; then there is at that moment kusala citta instead of akusala citta. However, nobody can cause the arising of paññā by striving to have strong concentration on particular objects one selects. There will be more detachment from the self if one does not sit down in order to concentrate on particular nāmas and rūpas and if one does not "plan" to have understanding. It depends on conditions whether or not there will be paññā. It depends on conditions what will be the object of paññā, it may be akusala citta or any other object. If we believe that by means of the development of understanding a great deal of kusala has been accumulated already, so much so that akusala can be burnt up, we do not know ourselves. Do we realize the countless moments of subtle clinging or of ignorance, arising time and again after there has been seeing, hearing, smelling, tasting or the experience of tangible object? Do we know whether there is at this moment kusala citta or akusala citta after seeing?

People who have practised in a center find it difficult to develop understanding in daily life, they find daily life distracting. One should check what one's goal is, understanding realities or being calm and free from disturbances? Daily life can be the measure of our understanding. When paññā is truly paññā it can understand as it is seeing occurring now, hearing occurring now, it can understand them naturally, in daily life. Paññā does not develop rapidly or suddenly. We cannot determine that from now on paññā should clearly understand realities. Paññā develops when it discerns the dhamma which appears naturally, in whatever situation or place one may be. We may believe that it is difficult to be aware of realities while we are working, but the situation of our work is daily life and any reality which appears can be the object of mindfulness. Alan Weller wrote:

"I do not separate Dhamma from work. I think that one sentence concerning the Dhamma, spoken by Alan Driver, can be applied and be of value in the work situation: 'We know from our own lives that we do not always give help when help is needed.' This can encourage us not to be neglectful of kusala in our work situation. Understanding can be developed in whatever situation, at different levels too: at the levels of sīla, of calm and of insight.

There is no self who can cause the arising of any reality. We have to be so very patient to let understanding arise by conditions and forget the trying and the wishing for results."

We acquire from the scriptures many valuable reminders to

develop understanding of nāma and rūpa. It is right understanding which should be emphasized, not concentration or effort. When understanding develops naturally, in daily life, there
are also concentration and effort or energy accompanying paññā,
they are cetasikas which perform their own functions. If we think
of concentration and effort there can easily be attachment, or,
when we worry about lack of concentration, there is aversion.
Someone asked Acharn Sujin whether he would have to stop
reading in order to be aware of different realities. He was wondering how paññā could know different realities while he was
reading. Acharn Sujin asked him whether during the time he
was paying respect to the Buddha, the Dhamma and the Sangha
and reciting the Pāli texts, he could, in between, also think of
other things. There can be many moments of ignorance in between, and thus, ignorance can arise extremely rapidly. Evenso
when paññā has been developed it is extremely fast. We underestimate the power of paññā. Paññā is different from what we
think it is. We are full of the idea of self and thus we imagine
that paññā can only know something if we first focus on it and
exert effort. We may think that it is not possible for paññā to
know the difference between sense-door process and mind-door
process , since the different processes of citta run extremely fast.
However, it can be known by paññā when it is developed to the
level of direct understanding. Or we may mistakenly think that
there cannot be sati and paññā in a sense-door process. Also
in sense-door processes there are conditions for akusala cittas
or kusala cittas. When there are kusala cittas they can be accompanied by paññā or unaccompanied by paññā, depending on
conditions. Nobody can tell paññā to arise or not to arise, nobody can predict the object of paññā. When it arises it performs
its function of understanding.

The rūpas which are the different sense objects are experienced through their corresponding sense-doors and then through
the mind-door. We may have doubts about this. We may be-

lieve that through the mind-door there can only be thinking
about concepts and not the experience of rūpas. We read in the
"Atthasālinī " (I, part II, Analysis of Terms, 72-74) that sense
objects are experienced through the senses and then through the
mind-door. We read about the javana cittas arising in a sense-
door process and then in the mind-door process:

> . . . Thus the javana cittas experiencing visible object
> arise at the eye-door and also at the mind-door. The
> same is the case with the javana cittas experiencing
> sound and the other sense objects . . .

The "Atthasālinī" states in the section on rūpa (II, Book II,
Rūpa, the four Great Essentials, 304) that the cognition through
the mind-door "falls into the stream of the fivefold cognition and
goes along with it." The mind-door process which succeeds the
sense-door process falls into its stream since cittas succeed one
another very rapidly. The rūpa is experienced through the sense-
door and then through the mind-door. When it is experienced
through the mind-door it has only just fallen away. During other
mind-door processes cittas can have as object a concept, such as
the shape and form of something.

The eye-door process, the ear-door process and the other
sense-door processes are each followed by a mind-door process,
but there are bhavanga-cittas in between the processes. Now,
at this moment, the different sense-doors are mixed up, they do
not seem to be demarcated by a mind-door process. It seems
that seeing does not fall away and that there can be hearing
or the experience of tangible object at the same time. This
shows us that processes of citta succeed one another very rapidly.
The mind-door is hidden at this moment, it is hidden by the
sense-doors. In order to remind us of what we do not know
yet Acharn Sujin said: "One door is bright, the other doors are
dark." Only when there is seeing the world is bright. But now

it seems that the world keeps on being bright. There seems to be seeing continuously.

At this moment we know in theory that nāma is the element which experiences and that rūpa is the element which does not experience anything. However, when, for example, there is the experience of heat through the bodysense, it is difficult to distinguish nāma from rūpa. There can be understanding of only one object at a time, either a nāma or a rūpa, and at that moment there is not "my body". When we think of "bodily sensations" we think of a "whole" and we are thoroughly mixing up nāma and rūpa. Then we shall continue to cling to a "self".

In the Tipiṭaka we read time and again about satipaṭṭhāna, the development of direct understanding of nāma and rūpa, and in the "Visuddhimagga" the different stages of insight, vipassanā, have been explained. We should not forget that direct understanding of realities could not arise if there were no intellectual understanding of the reality appearing at this moment, such as hardness, seeing or feeling. If intellectual understanding, pariyatti, is not firm enough there are no conditions for direct understanding, paṭipatti. We cannot tell when there will be paṭipatti, but it may take many lives. It should not matter, since whatever arises is non-self. When we read about satipaṭṭhāna and vipassanā, we can be reminded that the development of paññā is very gradual.

It is useful to learn some details about vipassanā and the stages of its development because it can prevent misunderstandings that may arise concerning the development of paññā. One may believe that there is already direct awareness of realities when there is only thinking about them. Some people believe that they can experience the arising and falling away of nāma and rūpa without knowing precisely what nāma is and what rūpa. Or they believe that they can discern the difference between the sense-door and the mind-door, whereas this is only realized at the first stage of insight. When one has such misun-

derstandings and one clings to what one mistakenly believes to
be vipassanā, one is not on the right Path.

We may have doubts about the characteristic of nāma and
of rūpa, but it is helpful to know that pariyatti is not yet firm
enough and that we should continue to develop understanding
of whatever reality appears.

Acharn Sujin gave several explanations about the stages of
insight but we should not cling to insight, then we are on the
wrong Path. Acharn said:

"The characteristic of nāma can only clearly appear when
the mind-door appears. At the moment of the first vipassanā
ñāṇa, paññā knows the characteristic of nāma and the characteristic of rūpa. Rūpa is not different from rūpa which usually
appears through the sense-door. Visible object appears through
the mind-door just as naturally as when we see now, but at that
moment it is not experienced through the eye-door but through
the mind-door."

During a trip in the North of Thailand Alan Driver asked
Khun Sujin some questions about the first stage of insight, vipassanā ñāṇa, and I shall quote the conversation:

Alan: "Does visible object appear to be the same through the
mind-door as through the eye-door, or does it appear differently
at the moment of the first vipassanā ñāṇa?"

Acharn: "It is the same, exactly the same".

Alan: "In that case how can one know the difference between
seeing and the experience of visible object through the mind-
door?"

Acharn: "Now there are sense-door processes, and mind-door
processes do not appear. When the mind-door appears in the
case of vipassanā ñāṇa it is different from just now."

One may be confused as to the characteristics of nāma and
rūpa. There is ignorance of the nature of nāma that experiences
an object. One may think about nāma but the characteristic
of nāma is not directly understood. Nāma such as seeing is

completely different from visible object which is rūpa but their different characteristics are not distinguished from each other. Hence there is an idea of "I am seeing different things and people".

Vipassanā ñāṇa arises in a mind-door process of cittas. Nāma can only be known through the mind-door and rūpa can be known through a sense-door and through the mind-door. However, one should not think of doorways; just their different characteristics can be known when they appear. At the moments of vipassanā ñāṇa the different characteristics of nāma and of rūpa are clearly understood by paññā through the mind-door.

Acharn Sujin said: "One rūpa at a time and one nāma at a time appears and is understood through the mind-door. The world does not appear, there is no self, there is nothing else but nāma and rūpa which appear one at a time."

At the moments of vipassanā ñāṇa there is no more doubt about the different characteristics of nāma and of rūpa.

Does nāma clearly appear as an element which experiences something? When we realize what we do not know yet we shall not erroneously believe that we can have direct understanding of the arising and falling away of nāma and rūpa. This can only be realized at a later stage of the development of understanding. First paññā must be developed to the stage that it can clearly distinguish between the different characteristics of nāma and of rūpa.

We should be grateful to the Buddha for teaching us about all realities which naturally appear in daily life. Thus we are able to test the truth of what he taught. He taught that each reality arises because of its own conditions. For example, if there were no eyesense and visible object, seeing-consciousness could not arise. Eyesense and visible object are necessary conditions for seeing. The eyesense is the rūpa which is the physical base or place of origin for seeing-consciousness. Seeing arises at that base. Hearing-consciousness arises at the ear-base and each of the other sense-cognitions have their corresponding base. The rūpas which are bases (vatthus) arise and fall away, they do not last. The base for body-consciousness can be at any point of the body, inside or on the outside. When we think of "body sensitivity" we still have an idea that the body itself can experience something. The bodysense is the base for body-consciousness and also for the accompanying bodily feeling which can be painful or pleasant. We dislike pain and we attach great importance to bodily wellbeing. When we know what exactly the bodysense is it will help us to have less confusion about nāma and rūpa.

The word body sensitivity can mislead us, the bodysense cannot experience anything. It can be a condition for the experience of tangibile object, of softness, hardness, heat, cold, motion or pressure. There can be impingement only by one of these rūpas on one extremely small point of the body at a time, and then body-consciousness experiences that object just for a moment. That point of the body is then the body-base and the body-door, but it falls away immediately. When a characteristic of rūpa is experienced, such as heat, impinging on the rūpa which is then body-base, nothing else can at that moment appear at other parts of the body. These parts are as it were completely numb, they cannot be the base for body-consciousness and bodily feeling. Neither can seeing or hearing arise at the same time, since only one citta arises at a time experiencing one object.

My husband pushed one hand on his shoulder and one hand on his waist, and he thought that hardness could be experienced on two points at the same time. When we only think of the body as a whole and there is no awareness of one object at a time, we shall not know the truth. We are misled by saññā, the cetasika which is remembrance. When saññā remembers wrongly, not according to the truth, it seems that there is "my whole body". All the rūpas of the body arise and then fall away immediately, never to come back again. Since we hold on to memories of what has been experienced and has fallen away already we do not know the truth. There may be "attā saññā", wrong remembrance of self, and "niccā saññā", wrong remembrance of things as permanent. Do we still think that the whole hand can "feel" something? Then there is wrong saññā. Because of association of different experiences in the past, also in the recent past, we form up the idea of a hand which feels something.

In the Commentary to the "Book of Analysis" (the "Vibhaṅga", the Second Book of the Abhidhamma), in the "Dispeller of Delusion" (Sammohavinodanī , Classification of the Khandhas) it is explained that saññā is like a mirage which deceives us:

> Perception, saññā, also is like a mirage in the sense of being unsubstantial, and likewise in the sense of being ungraspable. For one cannot grasp it and drink it or wash in it or bathe in it or fill a pot with it. Furthermore, just as a mirage quivers and seems like the movement of waves, so indeed perception also, divided up as perception of blue, etc. for the purpose of experiencing blue, etc., shakes and quivers. And just as a mirage deceives many and makes them say: "This is blue, beautiful, pleasant, permanent. " So too in the case of yellow and so on. Thus it is like a mirage by deception also.

We may not have considered to what extent wrong saññā influences our whole life. We are misled by the outer appearance of things. When children play with dolls and toy animals they live in their own dream world which they take very seriously. When a toy is broken or is lost they cry. Is it not pitiful that we do not really grow up, but keep on playing in our dream world? Because of saññā which remembers wrongly we hold on to all objects which are experienced. We have a short happy time

with the five khandhas which arise, are present for an extremely
short time and then fall away. We cry about our losses.

We can begin to develop understanding of different characteristics of nāma and rūpa. The study of the Abhidhamma helps a
great deal to eliminate misunderstandings about different nāmas
and rūpas. When, for example, hardness appears that characteristic can be known as rūpa, not self. We should not try to
catch the place which is the body-base at a particular moment.
Then there is thinking instead of awareness of the reality which
appears. The rūpa which is body-base cannot be experienced
through touch, it can only be experienced through the mind-
door. This rūpa falls away immediately.

We read in the scriptures that realities are not self, anattā,
but anattā may only be a word to us. Does the reality which is
not self appear already through eyes, ears, nose, tongue, bodysense
and mind-door? If we still confuse the different doorways it
seems that people, houses and trees appear, and they seem to
be real. Seeing is one experience and it experiences only colour,
it has nothing to do with hearing or the experience of tangible
object. It is only when paññā has been developed to the degree of the first vipassanā ñāṇa that no world, no person, no self
appears, only nāma and rūpa.

When the different objects experienced through the six doors
are not clearly separated we tend to think for a long time about
what is not real. Then the object which is experienced is a
concept. We are obsessed by our thoughts and we cling to them,
and thus, there are still conditions for rebirth. The arahat also
thinks of concepts, but he has no defilements, for him there are
no conditions for rebirth. We read in the "Kindred Sayings" (II,
Nidāna vagga, Kindred Sayings on Cause, Ch IV, § 40, Will),
that the Buddha, while he was at Sāvatthī, said to the monks:

> "That which we will, monks, and that which we
> intend to do, and that with which we are occupied:

- this becomes an object for the persistence of consciousness. The object, being there, becomes a basis for consciousness. Consciousness being based and having grown, there comes a bending; there being a bending, there is a going to a coming; there being a going to a coming, there is decease and rebirth; there being decease and rebirth, birth, old age and death happen in the future, and grief, lamentation, suffering, sorrow and despair. Even such is the entire mass of dukkha.

This happens also if we do not will, or intend to do, but are occupied about something. But if we do not will, nor intend to do, nor are occupied about something, these things do not happen. Even such is the ceasing of this entire mass of dukkha."

This sutta is about daily life. Time and again we are absorbed in our thinking and planning and there is forgetfulness of realities. We plan what we are going to do today or tomorrow. However, if there were no citta which thinks we could not plan anything. If we remember this there can be conditions for understanding of the citta which thinks and it can be known as a conditioned nāma. At that moment we are not obsessed by our thinking. There will be thinking again and again because there are conditions for it, but right understanding can know it as anattā.

Letter 4

Applications of mindfulness

We read in the "Kindred Sayings" (I,Sagāthā vagga, Ch IV, Māra, 2, par. 7, The Sphere of Sense) that the Buddha taught the monks about the six spheres of contact. Māra wanted to confuse the monks and therefore he made a terrible noise so that they thought that the earth was splitting open. The Buddha told the monks that it was only Māra. He addressed Māra in a verse:

> Sights, sounds, and tastes and smells and tangibles,
> All sense impressions and mental objects,
> These are the direful bait that draws the world;
> Herein the world infatuated lies.
> All this if he get past and leave behind,
> The Buddha's follower, with heedful mind,
> Passing beyond the range of Māra's might,
> Like the high sun fills the world with light.

We then read that Māra was sad and disappeared.

We are engrossed in the sense objects, but through the development of right understanding we can pass beyond the range of Māra. According to the commentary to this sutta , the "Saratthappakāsinī", the range of Māra are the three classes

41

of planes where one can be reborn: the sensuous planes, the rūpa-brahma planes and the arūpa-brahma planes. When there is no more rebirth one escapes the snare of Māra.

We are born in the human plane which is a sensuous plane. Our birth in the human plane is conditioned by kusala kamma performed by cittas of the sense sphere, kāmāvacara cittas. In the human plane there are opportunities time and again to experience sense objects. We are engrossed in all the sense objects and we keep on thinking about them. All these objects can only appear because there are cittas arising in processes which experience objects through the six doors. We may have learnt this through the study of the Abhidhamma but since we are so absorbed in the objects themselves we forget to consider citta, the reality which experiences them. The Abhidhamma teaches us about daily life and thus the study of it can motivate us to find out more about all realities which occur in our daily life.

When visible object impinges on the eyesense there are conditions for seeing, but visible object appears only for an extremely short moment. It is the same with sound and the other sense objects, they are all insignificant dhammas, they appear just for a short moment and then they fall away. Also the cittas which arise in the different sense-door processes and experience the objects fall away very rapidly. Cittas arise and fall away but each citta is succeeded by the next citta and thus it seems that citta can stay. After the experience of visible object, sound and the other sense objects, we form up concepts on account of these objects. Our world seems to be full of people and things and we keep on thinking about them. We are quite occupied with thinking and we take our thoughts very seriously. However, thinking only occurs because citta arises, thinks about something and then falls away.

Each citta experiences an object, and the object can be an absolute or ultimate reality, a nāma or rūpa, or a concept. We cannot predict which object will impinge the next moment on which doorway. Visible object, sound or the other sense objects can be pleasant or unpleasant. The experience of pleasant sense objects or unpleasant sense objects is vipākacitta which is conditioned by kusala kamma or akusala kamma performed in the past. There isn't anybody who can control vipāka. Vipākacittas just experience the pleasant sense object or the unpleasant sense object, they do not like or dislike it. At the moments of like or dislike akusala cittas arise. After the moments of vipākacittas there are, in the case of non-arahats, seven akusala cittas or kusala cittas which experience the object. When akusala cittas arise there is unwise attention to the object and when kusala cittas arise there is wise attention to the object.

We can notice that we all have different inclinations and these are conditioned by what has been accumulated in the past. Kusala citta and akusala citta arise and then fall away, but the succeeeding citta carries on to the next moment the inclination to kusala or to akusala and thus, there are conditions for the arising of kusala citta or akusala citta later on. Kusala citta and akusala citta of the past condition the arising of kusala citta and akusala citta at the present, and the arising of kusala citta and akusala citta at the present are in their turn conditions for the cittas arising in the future.

If our reactions today are conditioned by past accumulations it may seem that a fate reigns over our life. Someone was wondering whether there is no possibility to control one's inclinations, to exert effort for the development of kusala. The inclinations which have been accumulated in the past condition cittas which arise today but this does not mean that inclinations cannot be changed. If we listen to the Dhamma as it is explained by the right friend in the Dhamma, and if we study the Dhamma and consider it carefully, there are conditions for the arising of understanding of realities that appear. Right understanding must be developed from life to life but there is no self who develops it. The development of understanding depends on conditions. If there were no conditions how could it arise and develop? We are used to an idea of self who can exert effort but there is no one. We read in the "Visuddhimagga" (XVI,90) :

> Mere suffering exists, no sufferer is found;
> The deeds are, but no doer of the deeds is there;
> Nibbāna is, but not the man who attains it;
> Although there is a path, there is no goer.

There is a path and it can be developed but there is no self who can develop it. If right understanding is not developed there will be no end to clinging to the "self" and other defilements. We will continue being in the cycle of birth and death. We read in the "Kindred Sayings" (III, Khandha vagga, Middle Fifty, Ch V, par. 99, The Leash) that the Buddha said at Sāvatthī:

> "Just as, monks, a dog tied up by a leash to a strong stake or pillar, keeps running round and revolving round and round that stake or pillar, evenso, monks, the untaught manyfolk ... regard body as self, regard feeling, perception, activities, consciousness as self ... they run and revolve round and round from body to body, from feeling to feeling, from perception to perception, from activities to activities, from consciousness to consciousness ... they are not released therefrom, they are not released from rebirth, from old age and decay, from sorrow and grief, from woe, lamentation and despair ... they are not released from dukkha, I declare..."

We then read that the ariyan disciple who does not take any reality for self is released from dukkha. In the following sutta, "The Leash" II, we read again about the simile of the dog which is tied to a stake:

> "Just like a dog, monks, tied up by a leash to a
> strong stake or pillar- if he goes, he goes up to that
> stake or pillar; if he stands still, he stands close to
> that stake or pillar; if he squats down, he squats close
> to that stake or pillar; if he lies down, he lies close to
> that stake or pillar."

Those who take the five khandhas for self are like that dog which is tied down. They are always close to the five khandhas, they are tied down to it. A dog tied to a pole, which runs around it and always has to stay close to it, is a pitiful sight. So long as we take the khandhas for self we are not free. Through the development of right understanding the idea of self can be eradicated.

The Buddha taught the four "Applications of Mindfulness": mindfulness of body, of feelings, of cittas and of dhammas. Some people think that they should select one of these subjects, such as body or feelings, and only develop understanding of these. However, any object as it naturally appears in daily life can be the object of right understanding. If we try to select an object there is an idea of self who can control the appearance of particular objects. It depends on conditions whether visible object, sound, akusala citta or any other object appears. We do not have to make an effort to classify the object as one of the four Applications of Mindfulness. At one moment rūpa may appear, the next moment citta or feeling; nobody can predict which object will be the object of right understanding. We should learn that all realities are anattā, they cannot be directed by a self.

The Buddha taught the four "Applications of Mindfulness" in order to remind us to be aware and develop understanding of different kinds of nāma and rūpa as they naturally appear in our daily life.

We read in the "Kindred Sayings" (V, Kindred Sayings on the Way, Ch VII, par. 9, Feelings) that the Buddha said, while he was at Sāvatthī:

> Monks, there are these three feelings. What three?
> Feeling that is pleasant, feeling that is painful, feel-
> ing that is neither pleasant nor painful. These are
> the three. It is for the full comprehension of these
> three feelings that the ariyan eightfold Path must be
> cultivated.

In order to fully understand feeling there must be awareness
of the characteristics of all the different kinds of nāma and rūpa
which appear in daily life. Then right understanding of realities
can grow. Feeling is nāma, it feels, thus it is different from rūpa
which does not know anything. The difference between nāma
and rūpa has to be clearly discerned before paññā can realize
realities as impermanent, dukkha and anattā. The development
of the "Four Applications of Mindfulness" or satipaṭṭhāna is the
development of the eightfold Path. We do not have to think of
classifications while we develop the Path in being aware of any
object which appears.

Do we know feelings as they are? Feelings change all the
time since they arise and fall away together with the citta they
accompany. We may be aware of pleasant feeling or unpleasant
feeling, but we should also know the characteristic of indifferent feeling. When there is seeing the accompanying feeling is
indifferent feeling, there cannot be pleasant feeling or unpleasant feeling. When we feel pain we are inclined to think that
pain lasts. We think in this way because we do not realize the
different characteristics of realities which appear. When there
is impact of tangible object such as hardness on the bodysense
there can be conditions for painful feeling. Painful feeling accompanying body-consciousness which is vipākacitta only arises
for one moment and then it falls away together with the citta.
Tangible object which impinges on the bodysense falls away and
so does the rūpa which is the bodysense on which the tangi-

ble object impinges. We tend to forget that the bodysense on which tangible object impinges is only an extremely small part of the body, a rūpa which arises and then falls away. We keep on thinking of "my sensitive body". Right understanding reduces the importance of "my body" or "I". When we remember this we can read with more understanding what is written in the suttas about endurance. We read, for example, in the "Discourse on all the Cankers" (Middle Length Sayings I, no. 2) that the Buddha spoke about ways to eliminate defilements. We read about endurance:

> "And what, monks, are the cankers to be got rid of by endurance? In this teaching, monks, a monk, wisely reflective, is one who bears cold, heat, hunger, thirst, the touch of gadfly, mosquito, wind and sun, creeping things, ways of speech that are irksome, unwelcome; he is of a character to bear bodily feelings which, arising, are painful, acute, sharp, shooting, disagreeable, miserable, deadly..."

When one is wisely reflective one realizes unpleasant experiences as nāmas which arise because of their own conditions. Paramattha dhammas, nāma and rūpa, fall away immediately, they are insignificant dhammas, they are very trivial. We immediately form up concepts on account of paramattha dhammas which are experienced and we keep on thinking about concepts for a long time.

When we pay attention to the shape and form of things we think of concepts, but we could not think of shape and form if there were no seeing. Seeing sees colour or visible object but there is usually ignorance of these realities. They arise and then fall away but they are not known. Someone said that the word colour may be misleading, because when one recognizes red or blue there is already thinking. However, red or blue are seen without having to label them red or blue. These colours are not the same and they appear through the eye-door. If there were no eyesense the different colours could not appear. The "Dhammasangaṇi" (Book II, Ch II, 617) gives many details about colour. Colour can be blue, yellow, red, white, black, crimson, bronze, green, of the hue of the mango-bud, shady, glowing, light, dim, dull, frosty, smoky or dusty. It can be the colour of the moon, sun, stars, a mirror, a gem, a shell, a pearl, a cat's eye, gold or silver. The aim of giving so many details is to remind us to be aware of colour, no matter it is the colour of the moon, of a gem or any other colour. Also when we look at the moon or at gems there is colour and it can be known as the reality which can be seen. We do not have to make an effort to look for a special colour in order to be aware of it.

The "Dhammasangaṇi" gives in the same section (621) examples of different kinds of sounds:

> That sound which is derived from the four great Elements, is invisible and reacting, such as the sound of drums, of tabors, of chank-shells, of tom-toms, of singing, of music; clashing sounds, manual sounds, the noise of people, the sound of the concussion of substances, of wind, of water, sounds human and other than human, or whatever sound there is ...

Sounds are not the same, they are high or low, loud or soft, they have different qualities. We are so used to the familiar sound of the shuffling of feet, of the turning of pages or of pen or pencil when we are writing. We are usually absorbed in the meaning of sounds, thus, in concepts, but we can begin to understand the characteristic of sound. This is the way to know it as a reality which can be heard.

Patience and perseverance are needed for the development of right understanding. Life passes so rapidly, we are advancing in years and we do not know what our next life will be. We do not know whether we shall have the opportunity to develop paññā again, and therefore, should we not speed up our practice? We all may be inclined to think in this way, but do we realize that this is only thinking? We are so absorbed in the stories we are thinking of and are forgetful of the reality of citta which thinks. Thinking is a reality arising because of conditions, it is non-self. Lokuttara citta[1] cannot arise all of a sudden, understanding of realities has to be developed on and on. It has to be developed just now, not at some other time. Defilements are anattā, it is not possible to get rid of them quickly, they arise because they have been accumulated for aeons, they are conditioned. Only paññā can eradicate ignorance and wrong view. There is no need to think so much of effort, volition and concentration. Don't we usually think of effort, volition and concentration with an idea of self who wants to exert control? We may not attain enlightenment in this life, but what has been learnt is never lost. It has been accumulated and it can appear in another life. A moment of right understanding now, of our natural life, is more valuable than thinking of the future.

We read in the sutta "The Sphere of Sense" (Kindred Sayings I) which was quoted above, that the Buddha "was instructing, enlightening, inciting and inspiring the monks by a sermon on the six spheres of contact". This wording is also used in the previous sutta "The Bowl", and there the commentary (the Sarattha-pakāsinī) gives an explanation. The Buddha was inciting the monks so that they would apply the Dhamma. In this connection the Pali word "samādāna" is used, which means undertaking what one considers worth while. The Buddha preached to the monks so that they would consider the Dhamma and have right understanding. He instructed them so that they would have energy (ussaha) and perseverance for the application of the Dhamma. The Buddha taught about all the realities of daily life and these can be verified. The commentary explains that

---

[1] The citta which attains enlightenment and experiences nibbāna.

the monks were inspired, gladdened and purified because of the benefit they acquired from the Dhamma.

Acharn Sujin writes in her book "A Survey of Paramattha Dhammas" (Citta, Ch 16) about this passage in the commentary:

" . . . Someone may be unhappy and he may worry about it that he is growing older and that sati arises very seldom. When one worries the citta is akusala. We should not because of the Dhamma have akusala cittas, we should not be worried. The Buddha taught the Dhamma in order that people would be encouraged to apply it, develop it with perseverance and be inspired by it. Akusala arises when there are conditions , there is no self who can prevent its arising. When akusala citta has already arisen, we should not be downhearted, but we can take courage if there can be awareness of the characteristic of akusala which appears. One will not be troubled about akusala if one does not take it for self."

The monks were inspired and gladdened because of the benefit they acquired from the teachings. The Commentary adds: "We all can attain this benefit." We can really benefit from the teachings when satipaṭṭhāna is developed. The development of understanding of realities should not make us discouraged. The realities which appear can be penetrated and realized as they are. They arise and fall away, they are not self, not a being or person. When we consider the great value of the truth and know that we can realize it one day, although not today, we shall not be disheartened. One should not worry about it that one cannot know realities as they are today. Understanding can develop very gradually and then the characteristics of realities will surely one day be wholly penetrated and clearly known as they are.

When we see that the truth of Dhamma is for our benefit and that it can be attained, we shall not become discouraged. We shall continue to listen and to study the realities the Buddha taught in detail, and then we shall not be forgetful of realities, there will be conditions for knowing realities as they truly are.

Letter 5

Listening to Dhamma

We are disturbed by aversion, dosa, which often arises in a day
and we would like to get rid of it. We would like to have more
patience in difficult circumstances and more loving kindness towards others, but kusala citta does not arise very often.

If we want to cultivate patience and loving kindness, we
should see the disadvantage not only of dosa but also of all other
kinds of akusala. We find it unpleasant to have dosa, but dosa
is conditioned by attachment, lobha. Our attachment to pleasant objects conditions dosa when we do not get what we want.
There are many moments of akusala we are ignorant of. We may
notice that there is akusala citta when we act or speak in an unpleasant way, but countless moments of thinking arise which are
akusala and these pass unnoticed.

In which way do we think of others, with kusala citta or
with akusala citta? For example, when we notice someone who
is dressed in a peculiar way we may find him funny looking,
and we may have conceit. We compare him with ourselves; he
does not conform to the way we think someone should dress.
When conceit arises there is no loving kindness. When we are
annoyed about something which is very unpleasant we know that

this is dosa, but we may not notice dosa when it is of a lesser degree, for example, when something is not quite as it should be. Do we have kusala cittas or akusala cittas when we taste fruit which is overripe, when we see that a button is missing, when we feel a little too cold or too hot? We find it very important how the "self" is feeling. We only want pleasant objects and we forget that seeing, hearing and the other sense-cognitions are produced by kamma. We cannot notice kamma, it has been committed in the past, and nobody can change the result produced by kamma.

When we notice that there are so few moments of loving kindness, mettā, in a day and so many akusala cittas, we may become discouraged. However, there is no self who can prevent the arising of akusala and cause mettā to arise immediately. Akusala citta as well as kusala citta are nāmas which arise because of their own conditions, they are beyond control. It depends on one's accumulated inclinations what type of citta arises at a particular moment. Through the study of the Dhamma there will be more understanding of the different characteristics of kusala and akusala. The Dhamma is the condition for less ignorance in one's life.

If we want to develop mettā we must have a precise knowledge of its characteristic when it arises. At the moment of mettā we are not selfish, we only think of the wellbeing of someone else. There is kindness without expecting anything in return. Lovingkindness is one of the four "Divine Abidings", Brahmavihāras. The other Brahmavihāras are: compassion, sympathetic joy and equanimity. These are subjects of samatha or tranquil meditation. Also before the Buddha's time people developed samatha. They understood the danger of sense pleasures and by the development of samatha there could be temporary freedom from them. One may think that one has to go into seclusion in order to have concentration and that one should recite for example the "Mettā Sutta". However, the development of mettā is not a matter of trying to concentrate or reciting. Samatha cannot be developed without right understanding. The characteristic of true calm which is kusala should be known. Mettā can be developed in daily life when we are with others; then we can come to know its true characteristic. Foremost is right understanding which knows the characteristic of mettā when it appears. The "Divine Abidings" can condition moments of calm also when we do not intend to develop higher degrees of calm in samatha.

We read in the scriptures about people who developed samatha to the degree of jhāna, absorption, but we should know that not everybody is able to attain jhāna. People who had accumulated great skill for jhāna could attain different stages of jhāna, but, as the "Visuddhimagga" (Ch XII,7) states, jhāna is extremely difficult and only very few people can attain it. One has to live in seclusion and many conditions have to be fulfilled in order to attain it. At the moments of jhāna there are no sense impressions and the "hindrances" are temporarily subdued. The "hindrances" are: sensuous desire, ill-will, sloth and torpor, restlessness and worry, and doubt. However, through samatha defilements cannot be eradicated.

Only through right understanding developed in vipassanā defilements can be eradicated. We think of ourselves and others as persons, we cling to a concept of "self", but we can learn to see what we really are: only citta, cetasika and rūpa which arise and then fall away immediately. When someone goes away or dies, we can think of a name, but also a name is forgotten soon. We read in the "Sutta Nipāta" (on Decay, vs. 807-809):

> "As a man awakened from sleep no longer sees what happened in his dream, similarly one does not see a loved one who is dead. Those people who were seen and heard and called by their names as such and such, only their names remain when they have passed away."

When we are reborn there is another life and we are no longer

"this person", but also right now there isn't "this person" who
exists. We should consider what the conditions are for the physical phenomena we take for "our body". We have eyes and ears,
but we cannot notice what causes eyesense and earsense. It is
kamma, a deed performed in the past. The rūpas of the body
are conditioned by kamma, citta, temperature and food. We
are seeing and hearing time and again. Seeing and hearing are
cittas produced by kamma. They arise and then fall away immediately. When we think of other people we usually think of
names. We should consider the difference between names and
paramattha dhammas, absolute realities: nāma and rūpa which
can be directly experienced without having to name them. We
live mostly in the world of our thoughts, we keep on thinking of
stories about people, about their names, about concepts. However, we can learn to understand realities as they appear one
at a time through eyes, ears, nose, tongue, bodysense or mind-
door. Then we shall eventually be able to see realities as they
are: impermanent, dukkha and anattā. When we look at a chair
it does not seem to fall away. A chair is a concept we can think
of, but it is not a reality. Only paramattha dhammas have the
characteristics of impermanence, dukkha and anattā which can
be realized by paññā when it has been developed.

The object of right understanding of the level of satipaṭṭhāna
are paramattha dhammas as they appear one at a time through
one of the six doors. The object of samatha is one of the meditation subjects and the aim is to have true calm, temporary
freedom from akusala. Mettā, loving kindness, is an object of
samatha, but it can and should be developed in daily life. Mettā
is directed towards a person, thus, its object is not a paramattha
dhamma but a concept. There are many moments that we think
of people and instead of thinking with attachment, aversion or
conceit, we can learn to think with kindness. Mettā is a reality
and thus it can be object of understanding, it can be known as a
kind of nāma which is not self. Mettā is one of the "perfections"

(paramīs) which should be developed together with paññā from life to life. Through the development of mettā we learn to be less selfish and thus also mettā is, together with all the other sobhana cetasikas which are accumulated, a supporting condition for paññā which can eventually eradicate the wrong view of self. We cannot cause the arising of metta at will; we can learn to see mettā as a conditioned reality, not self.

Some people think that they should first have calm as a condition for more moments of satipaṭṭhāna later on, but that is desire, not mahā-kusala citta accompanied by paññā. Someone wrote to me that the development of jhāna would be beneficial for the development of vipassanā. He wrote:

"Jhāna can provide a very strong basis of concentration serving the development of insight. Though jhāna is not strictly necessary to develop vipassanā, it can prove very effective in suppressing the hindrances and thereby allows the development of insight to proceed with special strength and consistency. Jhāna fulfills the factor of right concentration in the noble eightfold Path."

The factors of the eightfold Path must be accompanied by right understanding of the eightfold Path, and the object must be a nāma or a rūpa. The factors of the eightfold Path are cetasikas which each have their own function in the development of right understanding of paramattha dhammas, of the realities appearing right now. When right understanding arises of the reality which appears there is also right thinking, vitakka, which assists right understanding; it "touches" the object which appears so that paññā can penetrate its characteristic and know it as it is. At that moment also right effort arises, which is effort or energy to develop understanding of the object which appears; it strengthens and supports paññā. The path-factor right mindfulness is aware of the nāma or rūpa which appears so that right understanding can develop. Right concentration (sammā-samādhi) is concentration on the paramattha dhamma which appears, just for that moment. As to the factors which are sīla (morality), namely, right action, right speech and right livelihood, they arise one at a time, when there is an opportunity for them. When there is a moment of right awareness and right understanding the eightfold Path is being developed.

The development of the eightfold Path is not a matter of developing concentration separated from the other factors of the eightfold Path. When right understanding arises of a paramattha dhamma which appears there is already right concentration which arises naturally, because of conditions. At that moment right understanding is assisted by the other path-factors and there is no need to think of path-factors or name them. If one encourages people to develop jhāna as a foundation for vipassanā many misunderstandings are bound to arise. People may not know what true calm is, they may not know what jhāna is. They do not realize that the objects of vipassanā and samatha are different. We read in the Visuddhimagga that jhāna can be a basis for the development of vipassanā. However, we should stress again and again that this can only be so when someone has the five masteries (vasīs, Vis. XXIII, 227): mastery of adverting and of entering jhāna at any time, at any place, resolving on its duration, emerging at any time, at any place and reviewing the jhāna-factors[1] at any time, at any place. Only then the jhānacitta can arise so naturally, that it is a reality of one's life and can hence be object of understanding. It can be a proximate cause or a basis for insight. But even those who have such skill cannot omit having clear understanding of paramattha dhammas, nāmas and rūpas appearing one at a time. The three characteristics of impermanence, dukkha and anattā of nāmas and rūpas have to be realized, no matter one develops jhāna or not.

We often read in the scriptures about people who developed jhāna and insight and then attained arahatship. Also before the Buddha's enlightenment people developed jhāna. The at-

---

[1] Specific sobhana cetasikas accompanying the jhānacitta.

tainment of jhāna is not specifically Buddhist, but the Buddha taught that one should not take jhānacitta for self. Therefore, for those who could attain jhāna, the jhānacitta should be object of satipaṭṭhāna. The Buddha spoke about jhāna because he included everything in his teaching, for completeness, for the beautifying of the teaching. He took account of all kinds of temperament.

I have noticed that people are inclined to stress concentration, also when they do not intend to develop jhāna first. They think that there must be a purified concentration by suppressing the hindrances first and that this would lead to uninterrupted mindfulness. However, defilements should be known as they are, as not self, that is the only way leading to their eradication. Seeing should be known as only a nāma, and also akusala citta which is likely to follow seeing immediately should be known as a kind of nāma. Is there not time and again like or dislike of the different objects appearing through the six doors? Should these not be known as they are? We should not remain ignorant of the akusala arising on account of the objects appearing through the six doors.

We read in the "Kindred Sayings" (V, Mahāvagga, Kindred Sayings on the Way, Ch VIII, par. 7, Hindrances):

> "Monks, there are these five hindrances. What five? The hindrance of sensual desire, the hindrance of malevolence, the hindrance of sloth and torpor, the hindrance of restlessness and worry and the hindrance of doubt and wavering. These are the five hindrances. It is for the full comprehension, realization, wearing down and abandoning of these five hindrances that the ariyan eightfold Path must be cultivated."

In the beginning we cannot yet have clear understanding of nāma as nāma and of rūpa as rūpa. Generally people want to stress exertion, volitional control, doing this or that special technique first, before developing understanding of whatever reality appears at the present moment. From the beginning one should understand that realities are anattā. Seeing is anattā; it arises because kamma produces it, nobody can produce his own seeing. In its train there are immediately javana cittas which are either kusala or akusala, but mostly akusala. They have already arisen before one realizes it. They are beyond control, anattā. We know that seeing sees, hearing hears, but what about this moment? We learn about processes of cittas, but do these not occur now? Different things appear, but they could not appear if there were no cittas arising in processes. When we are fast asleep we do not know who we are or where we are, there is no house, no book, nothing appears. All these things appear as soon as we wake up. Realities appear already, we should not try to do anything about them.

Some people say, "I had to break off my meditation because of sickness, stress of circumstances or work." No, when understanding of realities is naturally developed in daily life one will not break off its development. I believe we should have more understanding of this moment, and then of another moment. It is of no use to think, "when shall I attain this or that stage of insight or enlightenment", it depends on paññā and the other sobhana cetasikas which have been accumulated; they can condition the arising of satipaṭṭhāna, direct understanding, when it is the right time.

The writer of the letter thought that one should not say that realities are "beyond control" and that one should not say that it depends on one's accumulations whether kusala citta or akusala citta arises. He was inclined to stress volitional control. He said that, although one cannot have absolute control, there must be effort and a certain amount of control, otherwise one would be a victim of fate, one could not do anything.

Alan Weller wrote about this subject:

"I think that time and again we need to be reminded of the uncontrollability of realities in order to develop awareness of whatever reality appears naturally. Otherwise there will be the idea of self having effort, energy, etc. When we hear the word uncontrollable it does not mean we are the victims of fate, but we have to carefully consider how to develop the Path. The understanding of the Dhamma is the condition for wholesomeness at different levels, not control. Each moment of being awake we accumulate either kusala or akusala. Considering the Dhamma more is the condition for accumulating more kusala, but that also depends on previous accumulation. It is better not to mind or care what reality is there, but to just understand it. This is for me the subtlety of the teachings. It is so necessary to consider a lot in order not to be misled by desire or the idea of self. The understanding of uncontrollability can help us to develop understanding and not to accumulate more ignorance. It can help us to be natural in our development of kusala. No matter how busy we are, kusala at whatever level can arise any time by its own conditions. This understanding can help us to be detached from our practice. We do not try. We can become patient with lack of results, with our akusala. The practice can become a very natural part of our daily life. We do not limit it by thinking of a certain place or situation, or by making effort now and then. Confidence in the Dhamma, a sense of urgency, concentration, these are different realities which work by themselves. They grow as the understanding of the Dhamma develops. There is no one besides these realities. This moment is either kusala or akusala, a keener understanding will realize this more and more deeply and this will lead to turning away from akusala. I learn to be more considerate in speech and actions, also as regards seemingly unimportant things, which are often overlooked in daily life, for example, not leaving dirty washing or cups around, since this is unpleasant for others. There are many examples like this so close at hand. Dhamma is in front of us all the time."

When I use the expression "beyond control" I do not mean a fate, I only want to explain that realities are anattā. People want to do many things, instead of understanding realities just as they naturally appear. If one really scrutinizes oneself is there not an idea of "I do it, I want to make progress" There must be, so long as we are not sotāpannas, and thus, we need reminders all the time.

When I say that it depends on one's accumulations of kusala and akusala what type of citta arises I do not mean that we are in a hopeless situation. If there were no accumulation, how could we learn to have more mettā, or how could satipaṭṭhāna be developed? It is not true that nothing can be done. We should consider the Dhamma and develop intellectual understanding of whatever appears now, so that there will be conditions for direct understanding, paṭipatti. Listening to the Dhamma conditions more understanding of one's life. However, some people may hear the Dhamma but it does not mean anything to them. Why? They have no accumulations for it.

If someone thinks that he is a hopeless victim of his accumulations and cannot develop understanding, it is a moment of thinking which is akusala. When he thinks, "I cannot", he thinks so because of his lack of understanding of conditions. He clings to an idea of "self who cannot". When right understanding is developed it can understand this moment only. Dhamma is subtle and intricate, one really needs to consider it carefully. All moments of consideration of realities are accumulated, they are never lost. Thus understanding can grow and grow, until the time has come for direct understanding without thinking about realities. Then another step has been taken. Nobody can plan or control the arising of the stages of insight and enlightenment. The wish to control realities leads one away from developing understanding naturally in daily life. Some people want to sit and concentrate first on breathing, or on rūpas of the body they believe they can feel moving. One may be inclined to do something else first, anything else except knowing the present moment. Thus it is understandable that some people like to stress volitional control more than paññā.

Volition, cetanā cetasika, arising with each citta, is like a supervisor of the accompanying cetasikas, but it supervises them only at that one moment that it arises together with them. It cannot call paññā to come forward when there is no paññā at that moment. There is kusala volition and akusala volition; there is volition arising with vipākacitta and with kiriyacitta (inoperative citta) and these volitions are different all the time. They are conditioned by the accompanying dhammas and in their turn they also condition the accompanying dhammas. Volition is not a factor of the eightfold Path. Viriya (energy) is, but it is energy or courage for being aware and developing understanding of the reality which is appearing. It must arise together with right understanding of the eightfold Path in order to perform its function, and it prevents one from becoming disheartened about the development.

When we read about striving we should not think of merely striving with the exclusion of the other path-factors. One may still cling to an idea of self who strives, who exerts control over one's cittas, although one understands in theory that realities are anattā. Some people have an idea of separating their "meditation life" from their daily life. They believe that, for the development of the eightfold Path, it is necessary to go into seclusion first in order to suppress akusala and to induce calm. One may be used to the idea of exerting control over one's cittas, but it should be remembered that realities arise because of their own conditions. When understanding arises of the reality appearing now, even if it is unpleasant or akusala, it is accompanied already by right effort which performs its function without an idea of self who strives. Right effort is nothing else but effort for understanding right now and it arises because of its own conditions. What would be the use of the study of the Dhamma if it would not lead to the aim which is right understanding of whatever reality appears. We are the frequent victims of our own accumulations so long as we are not arahats yet. Right understanding will finally lead to the elimination of akusala.

I think we should not become impatient or disheartened by lack of understanding, lack of kusala. Gradually conditions can be accumulated for the growth of paññā. Not by volitional control. Not by trying to make particular realities arise, special objects of awareness, or doing special exercises. It does not matter if the reality which arises is a hindrance, it can be known as it is and in this way understanding can grow. When we have more understanding of paramattha dhammas we can read the suttas with more understanding. We read about striving and self-control, but we shall understand the deep meaning of what is said: that these are sobhana cetasikas arising because of conditions. The teachings can be most helpful in reminding us to cling less to an idea of self who can develop understanding. We do not develop understanding, it develops.

Letter 6

The long way

The development of satipaṭṭhāna is the only way to know the truth of impermanence, dukkha and anattā . However, we should remember that satipaṭṭhāna cannot arise if intellectual understanding of the present reality has not become very firm. At this moment we confuse all the different doorways and we do not realize nāma as nāma and rūpa as rūpa; we cannot distinguish them from each other. Acharn Sujin said that we are too sick to be able to walk along the Buddha's Path. She reminded us that the wholesome qualities which are the "pāramīs", the perfections[1] must be developed together with right understanding; they are like vitamins which will give us the strength to walk the Path. The Buddha, when he was still a Bodhisatta, developed the pāramīs for aeons. We all need the perfection of resolution aditthāna), which is the resolution to continue developing understanding of the nāma or rūpa appearing right now.

---

[1] The wholesome qualities which the Bodhisatta developed during countless lives and which were conditions to attain Buddhahood. They are: generosity (dāna), morality(sīla), detachment (nekkhamma), energy (viriya), wisdom (paññā), patience (khanti), truthfulness (sacca), resolution (aditthāna), loving kindness (mettā) and equanimity (upekkhā).

We know that the Path is difficult and that it will take many
lives to develop it and therefore, we need the firm resolution
to continue on. When we come to know more our akusala we
shall understand that defilements are deeply rooted. Akusala is
like weed which is deeply rooted and not easily pulled out. We
need the perfection of wisdom; it is right understanding which
can pull out the roots of lobha, attachment, dosa, aversion, and
moha, ignorance. We need the perfection of energy or courage,
viriya, so that we shall not become downhearted when progress
is slow. The perfection of patience is important; we should listen
to the Dhamma with patience and consider it carefully, so that
we can develop understanding of realities in the situation of our
daily life. We need the perfection of loving kindness, mettā, that
conditions kusala citta when we are with other people or when
we think of them. When mettā arises we consider other people as our close friends, even when we do not know them, when
they are strangers to us. We shall think of ways and means to
help them and to make them happy. It is natural that there are
people we do not find sympathetic, but when aversion or anger
arises we should consider that characteristic. Then we shall see
more clearly that aversion is useless and we can be reminded to
develop mettā right now. For the development of mettā it is necessary to have right understanding of the different cittas which
arise. When someone else speaks unpleasant words to us we are
likely to have resentment, but when we see the value of kusala we
can gradually learn to refrain from retorting such words and to
forgive him. Forgiving is a kind of generosity, it is like handing
a gift to someone.

We may find that it is more difficult to develop mettā when
we are tired because then we are more easily irritated and annoyed. Although we see the value of mettā we do not have
enough confidence in kusala; we have no conditions for kusala at
the moment we want to have it. Acharn Sujin said that the idea
of self is in the way all the time. We attach too much importance

to the way we feel. Tiredness is no reason for being angry, we should develop mettā in order to think less of ourselves.

We need also the perfections of generosity, of sīla and of detachment or renunciation (nekkhamma) so that we shall be less selfish and more considerate for other people's wellbeing. All the perfections should be developed, they are a necessary support for the arising of paññā in our daily life. When there is patience we do not mind it if understanding develops only little by little. There is conceit when we believe that we should be "somebody with great wisdom". We should follow Sāriputta's example who compared himself with a dustrag, a useless rag without any value. If we do not consider ourselves "somebody", but rather a "nobody", it will prevent us from pretending, even to ourselves, that we are more advanced than we in reality are. We also need the perfection of truthfulness (sacca) to keep us on the right track. We have to be sincere, truthful to reality. Do we want to avoid knowing akusala? If we are ignorant of akusala we shall take what is akusala for kusala. We need to develop the perfection of equanimity, upekkhā, in order to learn to accept with kusala citta the vicissitudes of life. Praise and blame are only realities which arise because of their own conditions; in reality people are not the cause of praise or blame. When people do wrong to us we can develop mettā if we see the value of mettā. Instead of having aversion about people's bad points we shall try to remember their good qualities. If they have none we can have compassion or there can be equanimity. Equanimity can arise when we remember that the real cause of unpleasant experiences through the senses is not a person but one's own kamma.

We should carefully consider the different perfections and then we shall be reminded to develop them in our daily life, they are necessary in each situation. Acharn Sujin said that while she prepares lectures for the radio she needs many perfections, such as mettā, patience, energy and equanimity. When there is equanimity she does not feel hurt when people do not want to listen to her or when they criticize her.

The perfection of wisdom must be developed from life to life. We know that we should realize the difference between paramattha dhammas, namely, nāma and rūpa, and concepts. It is necessary to consider the difference between paramattha dhammas and concepts in detail, under different aspects, in our daily life. All such moments of considering are accumulated, they condition the growth of paññā, so that one day, we do not know when, direct understanding of nāma and rūpa can arise.

When we see, we think that we are in this world, a world full of people, houses and streets. When we hear, we think that we are in this world, we hear people, animals, cars. We think all the time of the whole wide world with people and things in it. In reality there is only one moment of seeing and one moment of hearing. Seeing sees just that which appears through eyes, visible object, and then both seeing and visible object fall away. After that we think of a person or of the whole world, because saññā[2] remembers. There is only one moment of hearing and then both hearing and sound fall away, but we keep on thinking about what was heard, because saññā remembers.

When we think of a person or of the world, the object of citta is a concept. As soon as we notice the shape and form of a person or a thing there is a concept of a "whole". Even when we do not think of names we can still have a concept as object. When we perceive a pen we know already a concept before we think about the name "pen". Children who cannot talk yet and who do not know the meaning of conventional terms which are used in language can know concepts of a "whole". When they grow up they learn conventional terms so that they can name different things. They can then understand which person or thing is referred to. The English word "concept" (in Pāli:

---

[2]Saññā cetasika, remembrance or perception, arises with each citta. It remembers or recognizes the object or marks it so that it can be recognized later on.

paññatti) stands for the idea which is the object of thinking as well as the name or term used to denote such an idea.

We should not try to avoid thinking of concepts; even the arahat thinks of concepts because there are conditions for thinking. The arahat does not cling to concepts but we are still clinging. We have not eradicated "attā-saññā", the wrong remembrance of things as "self". We cling to the general appearance of things and to the details. When we cling to the image of a man or woman we do not know the reality which appears through the eyes, visible object, and, thus, we know only a concept, not a reality. We do not only like the general appearance of things, we also like the details. We are attached to the trademark of clothing, of cars.

Someone wrote to me that conventional truth is still truth: citta, cetasika and rūpa constitute the whole of a person, a living being which really exists. He finds that at the moment we adopt the discipline of vipassanā, paramattha dhammas appear and at the moments we deal with our ordinary life in the world, conventional truth appears. There are conditions to think of concepts, of "wholes", we need conventional terms in order to communicate with other people. We should lead our daily life naturally, but we can develop understanding of citta, cetasika and rūpa in our daily life. One may believe that these are constituents of a whole, but where is that whole? It only exists in our thinking, it cannot be directly experienced. We think that we see people lifting their hands or walking, but in reality there are countless nāmas and rūpas arising and falling away. So long as we do not realize the arising and falling away of nāma and rūpa, we cling to the idea that what appears are people, women or men, or this or that thing. We cling to the concept of somebody or something.

Acharn Sujin writes in "A Survey of Paramattha Dhammas", in the section on "Concepts":

"In order to know that concepts are not paramattha dhammas one should learn to discern the characteristics of the dif-

ferent paramattha dhammas which arise together. One should
be aware of one characteristic at a time as it appears through
one doorway at a time. The arising and falling away should be
realized of rūpa which appears through one doorway at a time,
so that the truth can be known. Each rūpa lasts only as long
as seventeen moments of citta and then it falls away. Therefore,
rūpa which arises has no time to stand, walk or do anything.
During the time one lifts one's hand already more than seventeen moments of citta[3] have passed. One sees people walking or
lifting their hands but in reality the rūpas which arise fall away
immediately and are succeeded by other rūpas. The rūpa which
is visible object appears to cittas of the eye-door process and
then, after there have been bhavanga-cittas in between, there
are many mind-door processes of cittas. That is why one can
see people walking or lifting their hands. Seventeen moments
of citta pass away extremely rapidly. Thus, one should consider
what happens in reality. One should know that the rūpa which
appears at this moment through the eyes only lasts seventeen
moments of citta and that it must fall away before sound can
be experienced through ears. It seems that there can be hearing
and seeing at the same time, but in between the moment of hearing and the moment of seeing there is an interval of more than
seventeen moments of citta. The visible object which appears
through the eyes and lasts seventeen moments of citta must have
fallen away before the citta which hears arises.

It seems that there can be hearing and seeing at the same
time, but these are different moments of citta experiencing different objects. Rūpas arise and fall away and succeed one another.
Visible object appears through the eye-door and after there have
been bhavanga-cittas in between it appears through the mind-
door. Then there are many mind-door processes of cittas which

---

[3]Rūpa does not fall away as rapidly as citta, but it still falls away very
rapidly. Comparing the duration of rūpa with the duration of citta it has
been explained that rūpa lasts as long as seventeen moments of citta.

think of concepts. That is why people who walk, lift their hands or move can appear."

We may have often heard that paramattha dhammas are not concepts and we may have repeated this for ourselves, but that is not enough. When right understanding of realities is developed we can learn when the object of citta is a paramattha dhamma and when there is thinking of a concept. It depends entirely on conditions whether a paramattha dhamma appears and there can be understanding of its characteristic, or whether one thinks of a concept.

We are inclined to cling to a self who develops understanding and we want to hasten the arising of the stages of insight. If we have such desire it hinders the understanding of realities as anattā. The stages of insight can only arise when there are the right conditions for their arising, not because we try to direct their arising.

Acharn Sujin writes about mindfulness in "A Survey of Paramattha Dhammas", in the section on the "Stages of Insight":

"Mindfulness is not easy and in the beginning it cannot often arise. The reason is that ignorance, clinging and all the other akusala dhammas have been accumulated for an endlessly long time in the cycle of birth and death. And also in this life, from the time we were born, defilements are being accumulated each day. When we correctly understand cause and effect of realities we know that we need great patience and perseverance so that we can listen to the Dhamma, study it carefully and consider it. Only thus can one have understanding of the realities which appear through eyes, ears, nose, tongue, bodysense and mind-door. When the right conditions have been accumulated for the arising of satipaṭṭhāna, the characteristics of the realities which are appearing can be investigated by being directly aware of them. Thus, eventually, realities will be known as they are. Through the practice one shall directly understand the truth in accordance with what one has learnt and understood intellectually,

namely, that all dhammas, and thus also satipaṭṭhāna and the
eightfold Path, are anattā. Satipaṭṭhāna can arise when there
are the right conditions, that is, when mahā-kusala citta accompanied by paññā has arisen time and again so that paññā can
be accumulated. Then we shall not deviate anymore from the
right Path. We shall not follow a practice which is other than
being aware of, noticing and considering the nāma-dhammas and
rūpa-dhammas which are appearing through the six doors."

We may pay attention to different realities and we may remember that seeing is nāma, that it is different from visible
object which is rūpa. The direct experience of nāma as nāma
and of rūpa as rūpa, without any idea of self can only be realized when intellectual understanding of whatever appears now
is well established. Nobody else can show us exactly how the
truth can be directly experienced, because paññā develops according to its own conditions. Seeing arises and we have learnt
that seeing is nāma, but so long as paññā has not eradicated the
idea of self, we still have an idea of self who sees. When paññā
has been developed to the degree that the first stage of insight,
vipassanā ñāṇa, arises, characteristics of nāma and rūpa appear
clearly, one at a time, through the mind-door. Their different
characteristics are clearly distinguished from each other. At that
moment there is no idea of self who experiences and there is no
idea of a "whole" or of the world. There is "anattā-saññā", the
perception of non-self, instead of "attā-saññā", the perception of
self. Only nāma and rūpa are appearing one at a time. If we really understand that there must be anattā-saññā at the moment
of vipassanā ñāṇa, we shall not try to create conditions for the
arising of vipassanā ñāṇa, because then there is an idea of self.
This would be counteractive to the development of vipassanā.

When the moments of vipassanā ñāṇa have fallen away, the
world appears as before, as it used to appear, as a "whole" or a
conglomeration of things, Acharn Sujin explained. We may be
surprised that realities appear as anattā only at the moment of

vipassanā ñāṇa, and that after that the world appears as usual, as a "whole". Has nothing changed? We may think that it is already an achievement to have reached the first stage of vipassanā ñāṇa but it is not enough. The accumulated clinging to a self is very persistent, it cannot be eradicated by the first vipassanā ñāṇa. One has to apply the knowledge one has gained at the moments of vipassanā ñāṇa and go on developing understanding of all nāmas and rūpas which appear.

It is only at the fourth stage of insight, which is the first stage of "principal insight",[4] that the arising and falling away of nāma and rūpa can be realized. Now, at this moment, hardness appears and is experienced, and both hardness and the experience of it fall away.

However, hardness is experienced again and again and it seems that hardness and the citta that experience it do not fall away. Each reality appears only once in the cycle of birth and death and then it disappears, it never comes back. When we meet people who are dear to us we should not forget that seeing only sees visible object and that seeing and visible object only last for a moment and are then gone for ever. "Everything goes, goes, goes", Acharn Sujin reminded us. It comes and then goes for ever. We may reflect on impermanence, but it is not the same as the direct experience of the arising and falling away of nāma and of rūpa. When the first stage of "principal insight" has arisen, vipassanā has become a "power" (bala)[5]

In the beginning, understanding of the characteristic of the

---

[4]The first three stages of vipassanā ñāṇa are beginning stages, they are called "tender insight", taruṇa vipassanā. The fourth stage is the first stage of mahā-vipassanā ñāṇa. Mahā means great. The objects of insight are the nāma and rūpa which appear, and as insight develops their characteristics are penetrated more.

[5]Specific cetasikas have been classified as "spiritual powers" which should be developed, namely: confidence, energy, mindfulness, concentration and wisdom (insight). When these have been developed so that they are unshakable by their opposites, they have become powers.

reality that appears is still coarse; there cannot be precise understanding yet. There is no realization of the characteristic of each
nāma and rūpa which appears one at a time, no realization of
their arising and falling away. Even at the first stage of principal
insight paññā is not keen enough yet so that there can be detachment from realities. At the second stage of "principal insight",
"Knowledge of Dissolution" (bhanga ñāṇa), paññā turns more
towards the falling away of realities and sees that they cannot
be any refuge. When insight has become already a "power" it
has become unshakable, but its development should continue on
so that there can be more and more "turning away" from nāma
and rūpa.

Knowing about the stages of insight helps us to understand
that paññā develops very gradually. We read in the "Path of
Discrimination" (Paṭisambhidāmagga, Treatise on Knowledge,
Ch XXXIV, par. 455):

> Insight power: in what sense is insight a power?
> Through contemplation of impermanence it is un-
> shakable by perception of permanence, thus insight is
> a power. Through contemplation of dukkha it is un-
> shakable by perception of pleasure ... Through con-
> templation of anattā it is unshakable by perception
> of self ... Through contemplation of dispassion it is
> unshakable by delight ... Through contemplation of
> fading away it is unshakable by greed ... Through
> contemplation of cessation it is unshakable by aris-
> ing ... Through contemplation of relinquishment it is
> unshakable by grasping, thus insight is a power.

It is unshakable, immovable and cannot be shifted by ignorance and by the defilements that accompany ignorance, thus
insight is a power. This is insight as a power.

Gabi wrote to me that she had read Acharn Sujin's "Stages
of Insight" with great pleasure:

"This shows with great clarity how intricate the development of satipaṭṭhāna is and how complicated it is. This does not discourage me at all, on the contrary, I enjoy it to take up time and again the scriptures and then I am reminded of the truth in my daily life. I am reminded that only paramatthas are real and everything else is only imagination."

In the commentary to the Therīgāthā , Canto XXXIV, Sukkā, we read that Sukkā had in many former lives listened to Buddhas, renounced worldly life, studied the Dhamma and explained it to others. Inspite of her great knowledge of the Dhamma she did not attain enlightenment. In this Buddha era she listened to the Buddha and when she heard Dhammadinnā preach she developed insight and reached arahatship. Once when she preached the Dhamma, a deva who lived in a tree was inspired by her words and incited people to come and listen to her. Sukkā, at the end of her life, declared her attainment in a verse. She called out her own name Sukkā , which means: bright, lustrous. We read:

> O Child of light! by light of truth set free
> From cravings dire, firm, self-possessed, serene,
> Bear to this end your last incarnate frame,
> For you have conquered Māra and his host.

This story shows us that it takes aeons to develop paññā. Even Sukkā who listened to several Buddhas needed aeons to develop the perfections together with satipaṭṭhāna. However, instead of wondering how arahatship could ever be achieved we can take note of the benefits of the development of understanding even now. Before we studied the Dhamma we did not know anything about citta, cetasika and rūpa. We did not know that on account of the pleasant or unpleasant objects experienced through the senses defilements such as attachment or aversion arise. Through the study of the Dhamma and through the development of understanding there will gradually be less ignorance

of the realities of our daily life. The development of right understanding takes aeons but even a moment of right understanding
now of a nāma or a rūpa is beneficial because it can be accumulated from moment to moment, from life to life. We should
not lure ourselves into thinking that through understanding we
shall have less aversion, dosa. First the wrong view of self has
to be eradicated and only at the third stage of enlightenment,
the stage of the non-returner, anāgāmī, dosa is eradicated. Because of the study of the Buddha's teachings we may notice that
there is aversion, for example, when we are talking and we have
unpleasant feeling. Then we are thinking about "our dosa", we
take it for self. We can learn to see defilements as conditioned
realities which are non-self. Also when we see the disadvantage
of akusala and we abstain from unwholesome speech, we should
remember that it is not self who abstains, but a type of nāma
arising because of its own conditions.

We read in the scriptures about Sāriputta's generosity, hu-
mility and gentleness. He had no anger and could forgive anybody. This can inspire us with confidence in the benefit of understanding which eventually leads to the fulfillment of all the
perfections. However, we should not forget that Sāriputta had
developed right understanding during countless lives until he had
eradicated all defilements. He had reached arahatship.

We read in the "Commentary to the Dhammapada" (XXVI,7,
commentary to vs. 389, 390) about Sāriputta's virtues. A brahman wanted to test his patience and therefore tried to provoke
his anger. When Sāriputta walked for alms he went behind him
and struck him violently with his fist in the back. Sāriputta said
"What was that?", and then, without turning around to look,
continued on his way. When the brahman became remorseful
and asked forgiveness, Sāriputta forgave him and accepted his
invitation to receive food in his house. We read in the Commentary that the monks were discussing this incident and were
offended about it that the brahman had struck Sāriputta. The

Buddha said to them:

"Monks, no Brahman ever strikes another Brahman;
it must have been a householder-Brahman who
struck a monk-Brahman[6]; for when a man attains the fruit of the third Path (anāgāmī or non-
returner), all anger is utterly destroyed in him."

We then read that the Buddha explained the Dhamma and
spoke the following stanzas, which are the verses 389 and 390 of
the "Dhammapada":

vs. 389. One should not strike a brahman; a brahman should not vent (his wrath) on him. Shame on
him who strikes a brahman! More shame on him
who gives vent (to his wrath). vs. 390. Unto a brahman that (non-retaliation) is of no small advantage.
When the mind is weaned from things dear, whenever the intent to harm ceases, then and then only
sorrow subsides.

When all defilements have been eradicated there is an end
to dukkha. There is no attachment and when someone else be-
haves in an unpleasant way one has no feelings of resentment,
no aversion. There is perfect calm.

---

[6]In the scriptures the word brahman is used in the sense of the person
who develops the eightfold Path leading to arahatship. The arahat has
eradicated all defilements.

Letter 7

The most valuable experiences

Dear Sarah,

Thank you for the tapes which you made in Bangkok when you and Jonothan were visiting Acharn Sujin. The discussions were in various surroundings: in the Safari Park, in the car, in a restaurant with loud background music, in a Park with a Japanese garden and in Acharn Sujin's house. The scenery changes all the time but there are only nāma and rūpa: visible object and seeing, sound and hearing and all the other realities. They appear but we need reminders so that we are not forgetful of what appears all the time. In your letter you wrote that you had carefully planned Dhamma discussions in the afternoon during the three days you were in Bangkok, but that things turned out quite differently from what you expected. Acharn Sujin was ill one of these days and thus she could not speak much. However, you had a good discussion with her sister and with Khun Duangduen. We make beautiful plans but we never know what will happen, because whatever happens is conditioned. Your letter was a good reminder of this truth. I liked Acharn Sujin's reminder: "Everyday life is a test for the development of understanding." We are in different circumstances, some pleasant, some unpleasant, but we should not forget that there are realities appearing through the six doors, wherever we are.

You spoke about the stress of everyday life people experience, when one is in the situation of one's work. It may be difficult to remember that there are only nāma and rūpa, and this is a problem we all have. When we are rushing around to finish our tasks such as cleaning the house or cooking, we believe that we need more leisure time, more time for reading suttas. But, as Jonothan remarked, do we really use our free time for Dhamma, or do we take up other activities, such as playing with the computer, solving problems with it? Different cittas motivate our activities, some are kusala but many more are akusala. They arise because of conditions, and instead of trying to exert control over them we should develop understanding of them. I liked Acharn Sujin's remark that we should not worry, that worry is akusala and that we should develop understanding at ease. I shall quote her words:

"...Develop at ease, don't rush. You should not want a result soon. One should understand one's own understanding. When there is a moment of not understanding it cannot be changed into a moment of understanding. When there is no understanding of visible object yet one can begin to develop understanding of it."

Acharn Sujin spoke about her daily life. She goes out shopping, she plays scrabble or receives visitors. She does not always read the scriptures, but she listens every day to Dhamma on the radio. She follows the Middle Way. We cannot exert control over the arising of understanding or direct it to specific objects. It is unpredictable what the next moment will be like. When attachment arises we can see it as just a reality. Acharn Sujin pointed out that we need many "ingredients" for the growth of right understanding. These ingredients are the sobhana cetasikas (beautiful mental factors) which have been accumulated and which support one another and cooperate so that right understanding develops to the degree that it can achieve detachment from the self. A cook needs many ingredients in order to compose a meal. In the same way many ingredients are needed for a moment of precise understanding of the reality which appears. It is necessary to accumulate many moments of reading, listening, studying and considering. When we study the Dhamma in detail, we collect ingredients which lead to direct understanding later on. Acharn Sujin said:

"We read in order to understand this moment.
We listen in order to understand this moment.
We consider in order to understand this moment."

I liked the discussion you had with Acharn Sujin about the importance of knowing details of the Dhamma. Some people may wonder why one should know details such as the four Great Elements of Earth, Water, Fire and Wind, which names designate the rūpas of solidity, cohesion, temperature and motion arising with each group of rūpas[1]. Is it not sufficient just to understand hardness when it appears?

Acharn Sujin answered that there are many realities appearing and that they are conditioned by different factors. Visible object is the rūpa which appears through eyesense, but visible object does not arise alone, it arises in a group of other rūpas in which also the four Great Elements take part. Visible objects are different because the four Great Elements which arise together with them are of different degrees. Detailed knowledge helps us to see that all that is experienced is conditioned reality. The more we understand conditions the more shall we understand that there is no self.

The study of the Dhamma is never lost, because the understanding acquired from it is accumulated, even from life to life.

---

[1] Rūpas arise and fall away in groups, consisting of at least eight rūpas, namely, the four great Elements and in addition colour, odour, flavour and nutritive essence. As regards the rūpas of the body, some groups consist of eight kinds of rūpa, and some consist of more than eight.

If we, in a next life, can listen to the Dhamma again there are conditions to understand the Dhamma more deeply. It is beneficial to know about the different cittas which arise in processes because this is our daily life. As Acharn Sujin said, we study in order to know this moment. We should not forget the goal of our study: detachment from the idea of self by right understanding. This understanding eventually leads to the eradication of all defilements. There is impingement of visible object, sound and the other sense objects on the relevant sense-doors and these objects are experienced by cittas which arise and fall away, succeeding one another in processes. In a process of cittas there are moments of citta which are either kusala or akusala, the moments of javana-cittas[2], but most of the time we are ignorant of this. On account of the objects which are experienced through the different doorways we form up long stories, we are quite absorbed in our thinking. The cittas which think arise in mind-door processes and they may be kusala, but most of the time they are akusala. We cling to the people around us or we are annoyed about them, and we forget that there are no people, only nāma and rūpa.

Acharn Sujin stressed during the discussion that when we go to sleep all the stories we made up during the day are forgotten. It is true that when I am asleep I do not know who I am, whom I am married to or where I live. We have forgotten our joys, fears and worries. When we are asleep and not dreaming there are no processes of cittas which experience objects impinging on the six doors. There are bhavanga cittas (life-continuum), cittas which have the function of keeping the continuity in life, and these cittas experience the same object as the rebirth-consciousness, which is the object experienced shortly before the dying-consciousness of the previous life. It is beneficial to know such details, it helps us to understand that

---

[2]Usually five cittas perform the function of javana, running through the object, and for non-arahats they are kusala or akusala.

all the stories we are absorbed in now are nothing at all. They exist only so long as we are thinking about them, but they are forgotten as soon as we are asleep.

Acharn Sujin said that we should not wait until we go to sleep to forget about the stories we make up. One can come to realize that the processes of cittas which experience sense objects pass like a flash and that on account of them there is thinking. We live in our own world of thinking from birth to death. We have different feelings because of our thinking, but everything passes like a flash, it is very temporary. After seeing thinking arises, and after hearing thinking arises. What we are used to taking for something permanent appears for a very short moment and then it is completely gone. We have heard this before but it is good to be reminded of the truth. Acharn Sujin remarked:

"In your idea it is as if things are permanent, but it all is so short, it is nothing at all. When one says, "life is so short", one should remember that each moment is shorter. It never comes back. We listen to the song of a bird but it is completely gone in split seconds."

When we are thinking about temporariness there may be moments of calm with impermanence as object. We know that we understand about impermanence in theory, that we can think about it, but we do not directly experience the truth. I quote your conversation with Acharn Sujin:

Acharn: "There can also be a moment of insight, of understanding realities which arise and fall away, but it depends on the development of understanding whether that degree has been reached or not yet. It is not a matter of wanting or trying, but of developing."

Sarah: "When we talk about stages of insight we start to worry. Why should we not just be aware of the characteristic which appears?"

Acharn: "People worry because they want to experience the stages of insight. One has to develop understanding. Then one does not worry about the different stages. One knows that one will reach them one day if the Path is right. One moment of understanding will lead to more understanding. There are only six doorways. Seeing continues from life to life. If one dies now and one is reborn for example in a deva plane, seeing follows instantly and it is like this from aeon to aeon. One sees a great deal and there is no understanding of seeing until one listens to the Dhamma and begins to develop understanding. There can be understanding of seeing as it is. If someone thinks that the development of understanding is too difficult and that he should do other things in order to have more awareness he does not see the value of a moment of being aware of a reality, of understanding it."

The following sutta reminds us that understanding does not develop by mere wishing, that it only grows by developing it right now. We read in the "Gradual Sayings" (Book of the Threes, Ch X, § 91, Urgent):

> "Monks, there are these three urgent duties of a yeoman farmer. What three? Herein, monks, the yeoman farmer gets his field well ploughed and harrowed very quickly. Having done so he puts in his seed very quickly. Having done that he lets the water in and turns it off very quickly. These are his three urgent duties.
>
> Now, monks, that yeoman farmer has no such magic power or authority as to say: "Let my crops spring up today. Tomorrow let them ear. On the following day let them ripen." No! It is just the due season which makes them do this.
>
> In the same way there are these three urgent duties of a monk. What three?
>
> The undertaking of training in higher sīla, in higher citta and in higher insight. These are his three urgent

duties.

Now the monk has no such magic power or authority as to say: "Today let my mind be released from the āsavas without grasping, or tomorrow, or the following day." No! It is just the due season which releases his mind, as he undergoes the training in these three.

Wherefore, monks, thus must you train yourselves: Keen shall be our desire to undertake the training in these three branches of training. That is how you must train yourselves."

There is higher sīla, higher citta (higher concentration) and higher insight when the eightfold Path is developed. We may keep on thinking that the realization of the truth is too difficult. If there is no development of understanding now defilements cannot be eradicated. We cannot hasten the development of understanding, but when we see that the development of the eightfold Path is the only way to eliminate ignorance there will be conditions for understanding the present reality.

We may wonder how to know the difference between kusala and akusala. We know in theory that they are different but we find it difficult to know directly when the citta is kusala and when it is akusala. When we help someone there are kusala cittas, but there are also akusala cittas with attachment to the person we help or with attachment to "our kusala". Cittas are very intricate and they change very quickly. Acharn Sujin explained that we can only know the present moment:

"If we do not talk about this moment how can we know whether the citta is kusala or akusala? It is helpful to know this in daily life. When you think of the other person's benefit without attachment there can be kusala at the level of dāna. People have kusala cittas in a day but they don't know it. Right understanding can understand that there are different nāmas."

Khun Duangduen had offered coffee to Jonothan and while she was thinking of his benefit without attachment the citta was kusala. Generally we worry too much about the development of kusala. Acharn Sujin remarked that some people think and think and think how they can have more kusala whereas others just perform it whenever there is time and opportunity. We keep on worrying about kusala and also about our akusala.

I noticed that Acharn Sujin stressed several times that one should not worry and that one should develop right understanding at ease. She repeated what she had said in India about her anger. She said that it is no problem to her when she gets angry since it has conditions for its arising. She does not think, "O, I studied a lot and therefore I should not have anger." Gabi had listened to the tapes which were recorded in India and she wrote to me about her reactions concerning this subject:

"I was so surprised when I heard Acharn Sujin say, 'I am not bothered by my dosa, I don't want to control it'. I was struck by these words and they made me have a totally new approach to dosa and anattā, not self. Acharn Sujin had often said, 'It is not your dosa', but this had not convinced me. Should one not work on oneself, should one not pull oneself together, and if one has the will to do this can one not succeed? Seminars are organised to help people with problems in relationship and to make them change their behaviour, and these seminars are successful. And now I hear from Acharn Sujin, 'I am not bothered by my dosa and I don't want to control it'. Why am I bothered by my dosa? Because the accompanying feeling is unpleasant and my fellowmen do not like me for it, or they do not admire me."

We cannot prevent thinking, but it is important not to forget that dhammas are anattā, beyond control. I think that one could say that Acharn Sujin does not want to control 'her' dosa and that she is therefore not disturbed by it.

That is the answer. When we realize that whatever appears is "only a reality", that it is conditioned, not self, we shall be less disturbed by it. This does not mean that we should not develop wholesome qualities. We notice that often akusala citta arises but instead of having aversion there can be a moment of understanding of what appears. Dosa will arise again but then there can be a moment of understanding of its characteristic. "One does not worry, one keeps on developing understanding", as Acharn Sujin said.

We think about awareness but we forget to attend to characteristics of softness or hardness which appear time and again through the bodysense. One hears about the characteristic of anattā but it does not appear. Acharn Sujin explained:

"When one begins to develop understanding there is no distinction between nāma and rūpa, they are all mixed up. Then there cannot be elimination of the idea of self from any reality. By developing understanding of realities one at a time one can learn that the reality which experiences now is just an element, that it is a reality different from visible object which is seen. If one understands this one will learn that there is nobody who experiences, and nobody, no thing in the visible object. It takes time to have clear understanding of visible object, seeing, sound, hearing, of all realities appearing through the six doorways.

When we notice people we can remember that this is the same as looking into a mirror, since only visible object is experienced and there are no people. We only make up our stories about people. We begin to see that it is visible object, not a thing or a person. Is this not a beginning of understanding of the nature of anattā of visible object?"

We may say that we see the value of right understanding but do we really mean it? The following sutta can remind us of what is most valuable in life. We read in the "Dialogues of the "Buddha" (Dīgha Nikāya III, The Recital, VI, 18):

Six unsurpassable experiences, namely: certain sights, certain things heard, certain gains, certain trainings, certain ministries, certain recollections.

This passage is short but deep in meaning and it will be explained further on.   Unsurpassable experiences are experiences which are superior, most valuable. The Pāli term used here is "anuttariya ". Achan Sujin explained the meaning of the six "anuttariyas" in the Bovornives Temple and quoted the "Manorathapūranī", the commentary to the Anguttara Nikāya (commentary to the Book of the Ones, Ch XIII). This commentary deals with the six anuttariyas.

The first unsurpassable experience is the unsurpassable experience of sight (dassana). Ānanda had this experience because he saw the Buddha the whole day and he had developed right understanding and attained enlightenment. If someone sees the Buddha but he does not develop right understanding he does not have the unsurpassable experience of sight. He does not really value the Buddha and his teaching. The commentary states that the other enlightened disciples and also the "noble persons" (kaliyāna puggala), namely those who developed the eightfold Path, had the unsurpassable experience of sight. We cannot see the Buddha now but we can apply what he said to Vakkali who was attached to the sight of him (Theragāthā 205). The Buddha said: "Who sees the Dhamma sees me".

As to the unsurpassable hearing (savana), Ānanda heard the Buddha preach and developed right understanding so that he could attain enlightenment. The same is said with regard to the other enlightened disciples and all those who developed the eightfold Path. They listened and developed satipaṭṭhāna so that they could attain enlightenment. When we listen to the Dhamma now and we begin to develop understanding we can have the unsurpassable hearing. We can come to realize that the explanation of the Dhamma is the most precious thing that can be heard.

What is the most precious gain (lābha)? Everybody wants

excellent things, but if there is no wisdom one does not know whether one's possessions are really superior. Those who had strong confidence in the Buddha, like Ānanda, had the best of gains. The same is said about the other enlightened disciples and the noble persons who developed the eightfold Path. We find the things which give us pleasant feeling most valuable in our life. However, the teachings remind us that pleasant feeling is very temporary, that clinging to pleasant objects leads to sorrow. When we have enough confidence in the teachings we shall continue to develop right understanding of all realities which appear. We shall see that it is most valuable to know our defilements, to have less ignorance about realities. Then we shall have the best of gains. As to the trainings (sikkhā) which are superior, these are the higher sīla, the higher citta (samādhi, concentration) and higher wisdom of the eightfold Path. Ānanda and the other disciples of the Buddha valued these three trainings as unsurpassable, since they lead to the eradication of defilements. If we see them as unsurpassable there are conditions to be less neglectful, to develop understanding of any reality which appears, pleasant or unpleasant, kusala or akusala.

The unsurpassable ministry (pāricariya) is the ministry to the Buddha, as Ānanda and the other disciples performed. Through satipaṭṭhāna they had acquired the greatest confidence and respect for the high qualities of the Buddha who taught the truth of impermanence, dukkha and anattā. Without right understanding the ministry to the Buddha is not an unsurpassable experience. The Buddha has passed away but we can still serve the Dhamma. One ministers to the Dhamma when one studies it and explains it to others so that they too can develop right understanding.

The unsurpassable recollection (anussata) is the recollection of the Buddha's qualities, those which are "worldly" (lokiya) as well as those which are supramundane (lokuttara), the commentary states. Without wisdom one cannot recollect the qualities of the Buddha. When understanding of the reality that appears at this moment is developed, we value the Buddha's wisdom at that moment. Without his teaching we could not develop understanding. Thus, at that moment there is the sixth unsurpassable experience.

Acharn Sujin said that enlightenment cannot be attained without these six most excellent experiences. If we do not consider the Dhamma as that which is most valuable in our life, enlightenment cannot be attained. We value the Dhamma not merely by words, but by developing right understanding. When we listen to the Dhamma, consider what we heard and begin to understand realities that appear we can verify the truth of what the Buddha taught. Then we can gain more confidence to develop all the "perfections", the good qualities the Buddha had developed together with right understanding during aeons. Ānanda and the other disciples had developed the perfections during aeons and when they met the Buddha and listened to him it was the right time for them to attain enlightenment.

With mettā,

Nina

Letter 8

Not selecting objects

The Hague,
June 29, 1991

Dear Robert,

You know that the eightfold Path the Buddha taught is the Middle Way. The Buddha said in Isipatana to the five disciples that two extremes should not be followed: devotion to sense pleasures and devotion to self-mortification (Kindred Sayings V, Mahā-vagga, Book XII, Ch II). We may understand in theory that we have to follow the Middle Way, but when it comes to the practice doubts may arise. Should we do particular things in order to have more understanding and should we avoid things which seem unfavorable for its development? We may do wholesome deeds such as performing generosity or helping others, but still, attachment, lobha, aversion, dosa, and ignorance, moha, arise time and again, and understanding seldom arises. We may become discouraged about our lack of progress. You have realized that understanding should be developed naturally, in daily life, but, as you wrote, you have doubts whether you should avoid certain situations. You mentioned that you had doubts

91

whether you should accept an invitation from your friends to go to the movies or whether you should stay home in order to study Dhamma. You feel that accepting is indulgence in pleasure. Nevertheless you find that, even while watching the movie, you would have the opportunity to face the present reality. I will quote from your letter:

"Although I have at home the opportunity to study the Dhamma perhaps there will be a feeling of "my practice", "my sīla", so that the benefits may not be high. Whereas if I would accept I would lose the study time but there is less chance of developing attachment to "my practice" and really just as much time to observe the present moment. I guess that the answer to this is that the practice is not so much to accumulate many kusala cittas but rather to develop understanding which recognizes the different characteristics of all rūpas and nāmas and sees them as anattā, including sati and paññā."

The answer to this dilemma is that one never knows beforehand which type of citta arises at which moment, kusala citta or akusala citta. Cittas arise because of their own conditions and there isn't anybody who could control them. Correct understanding of the "Middle Way" is knowing that whatever arises is a conditioned dhamma and that there is no person who acts in this or that way. There is no person, only citta, cetasika (mental factor accompanying citta) and rūpa.

Only the anāgāmī, the person who has realized the third stage of enlightenment, will never indulge in sense pleasures. He will have no inclination to go to movies. For us it is different. Sometimes we shall accept an invitation to go to the movies, sometimes we shall decline and the cittas arising in both cases can be kusala or akusala, nobody can predict that. We can also accept an invitation because of kindness, out of consideration for someone else who may not be able to go alone. How could one prescribe citta what to decide? Each citta arises because of its own conditions, it is anattā, beyond control.

Sometimes while watching a movie one can have understanding that what appears through the eyes is visible object, that which can be seen. When we are absorbed in the story we are thinking of concepts. The thinking is conditioned by seeing. When we stay home in order to study the Dhamma there may not be any understanding at all, how could it be planned? As you say, there can always be attachment to "my practice", but this is a conditioned nāma and it can be realized as such.

You have understood that our goal should not be merely the accumulation of kusala but rather the understanding of all realities, sati and paññā included, as anattā. Someone wrote that a teacher said to his pupils that there should be continuous mindfulness but how could one control mindfulness, causing it to arise and remain? It can only arise when there are the right conditions and when it has arisen it falls away immediately. We cannot help seeing and hearing time and again, these cittas just arise, whether we want it or not. Seeing and hearing arise in processes of cittas and in these processes there are, shortly after seeing or hearing has fallen away, kusala cittas or akusala cittas, but most of the time akusala cittas. Often we may not pay attention to seeing or hearing, they just pass. Also the akusala cittas which arise shortly after seeing and hearing just pass, we do not notice them. Cittas arise and fall away very rapidly. Therefore, it is hard to know whether the citta at this moment is kusala or akusala. You write that you are inclined to slip off the Middle Way. We all do, so long as we are not sotāpannas, those who have attained to the first stage of enlightenment. I quote from your letter:

"I am inclined to think, 'Well, the accumulations to enjoy are there. I might as well indulge as long as I know it is not self doing it, just desire arising'. But often I find that by going ahead and enjoying, somehow there is little awareness and more attachment. On the other hand, by suppressing the desire, such as by taking the eight precepts[1], a feeling of discomfort may be present. But this has the benefit of marking the defilement in a clear way."

Again, we cannot set any rule for citta what to decide to do at a particular moment. When we listen to the teachings and consider them we learn that all realities that appear are just conditioned dhammas. When we give in to enjoyment and think, "It is not self", it may be thinking with akusala citta or with kusala citta. There can be understanding that giving in to enjoyment is just a conditioned dhamma. It is conditioned by accumulated desire for pleasant objects.

You find that the eight precepts bring you discomfort. Nobody else can tell you to observe them or not to observe them. Do we cling to our own kusala, do we want to be perfect immediately? You may find that you notice your attachment to a soft chair or a soft bed more clearly when you take the eight precepts, but what about attachment after seeing or hearing now? Sincerity is indispensable for the development of understanding. One has to be truthful with regard to the different cittas which arise, be they akusala or kusala. They are just dhammas and nobody can do anything about them.

Understanding of realities can be developed by listening to the Dhamma and by considering them. Moreover, all kinds of kusala have to be developed as well, since the goal is the eradication of defilements. The wholesome qualities that are the "perfections" have to be developed together with paññā, right understanding of realities. If we learn about nāma and rūpa but we neglect generosity we will keep on clinging to the self. It is difficult to develop generosity when a great deal of stinginess has been accumulated, but we should get to know our true ac-

---

[1]Laypeople can, in addition to the five precepts, take three more precepts on special days such as the full moon day. These include not eating after midday, not using high and soft beds or chairs, not using adornments or perfumes.

cumulations. When we notice stinginess we do not like it, we have aversion about it. Or there is regret, kukkucca, about our akusala or about the kusala we omitted, and that is also akusala. The characteristic of stinginess can be realized as only a conditioned reality, a type of nāma. There can be more understanding of its conditions: it arises because it is deeply accumulated. We do not want to be stingy, we may tell ourselves not to be stingy, not to speak words which express our stinginess, but stinginess still arises.

We may come to know that there often is conceit in our relationship with others. We may feel displeased about what someone else is doing to us or saying to us. There is a kind of comparing, there is "he" and "me"; we wonder, "how can he do that to me." Then there is conceit, we cling to "our important personality". Conceit hinders generosity and mettā. Can we forgive someone else easily? Forgiving is a kind of generosity, dāna. It is "abhaya-dāna", the wish that someone else is free from harm. We should more often consider the benefit of forgiving, it helps us to have less conceit.

We may be inclined to blame someone else when we notice that he has akusala citta, we may want to tell him off. However, when we are sincere we can come to know our own akusala. Sincerity or truthfulness is one of the perfections that should be developed.

We read in the "Gradual Sayings" (Book of the Tens, Ch V, par. 4, At Kusinara) that the Buddha, while he was staying at Kusināra, said that a monk who desires to admonish another monk should do so after investigation of five conditions in himself and setting up five conditions in himself. We read that he should investigate whether he practises utter purity in body and speech, whether he has mettā established towards his fellow monks and is free from malice. If not, people around him will say that he should practise these things himself. We then read:

> "Then again, monks, a monk who desires to admon-
> ish another should thus investigate: Am I or am I not
> one who has heard much, who bears in mind what he
> has heard, who hoards up what he has heard? Those
> teachings which, lovely alike at the beginning, the
> middle and the end, proclaim in the spirit and in the
> letter the all-fulfilled, utterly purified Brahma-life,
> have such teachings been much heard by me, borne
> in mind, practised in speech, pondered in the heart
> and rightly penetrated by view? Is this quality man-
> ifest in me or is it not? Then, monks, if he be not
> one who has heard much ... if those teachings have
> not been rightly penetrated by view, then folk are
> found to say to him: 'Come now, let your reverence
> complete knowledge of the Sayings.' Folk are found
> to speak thus."

We then read that the monk who desires to admonish another monk should investigate whether he is well-trained in the
discipline. After that we read about five conditions which he has
to set up in himself:

> "(He considers:) Do I speak in season or not? Do I
> speak of facts or not, gently or harshly, do I speak
> words fraught with profit or not, with a kindly heart
> or inwardly malicious? These five conditions he must
> set up in his own self."

We can apply this sutta in daily life. It is very difficult to
fulfill the conditions the Buddha mentioned, and when we see
that, we may rather refrain from admonishing someone else.

Someone wrote that one should try to put as much kusala in
one's mind as one can. In that case there could be an idea of
self who is trying and one will certainly fail. The same person
was in a meditation center and he was hoping that he, in that

place, could have more mettā. However, he noticed that he could not. It shows that realities are beyond control, anattā. It can be discouraging to see how little mettā there is in a day. We used to take for mettā what is only attachment. We were inclined to be kind to particular people only, not just to anybody we meet. But it is helpful to realize that often attachment and conceit hinder mettā.

You spoke about "meditation life" and you thought that your meditation life was different from daily life, but, as you know now, that that is not the Middle Way. When we would just be sitting in a quiet room how could we know ourselves as we are in our daily life, in our work situation, in our relationship with others? We should be truthful and we should not pretend, even to ourselves, to be better than we really are.

The word meditation can create confusion. People associate meditation with going apart and trying to concentrate on something special. It is true, if one wants to cultivate calm to the degree of jhāna one has to live a secluded life and one has to use a meditation subject of samatha in order to make calm grow. For the development of right understanding of realities one does not need to go apart. One should develop it naturally, in daily life. One should come to know one's real accumulations, one's defilements. If one does not develop understanding of whatever reality appears paññā cannot grow.

You asked what the difference is between paññā in samatha and paññā in vipassanā. The aims and thus also the methods to reach them are different. As regards samatha, even people before the Buddha's time saw the danger of sense impressions. They realized that seeing, hearing and the other sense impressions are often followed by defilements. Therefore, they used subjects of meditation in order to reach jhāna, because at the moment of jhāna-citta there cannot be any sense impressions. By means of jhāna defilements are temporarily subdued but they are not eradicated. The aim of vipassanā is the eradication of defilements through the wisdom which knows all realities as they are.

Actually, we should emphasize again and again that vipassanā is direct understanding of realities and that this cannot
arise if there is not first intellectual understanding of whatever
reality appears now, pariyatti. Only when pariyatti is quite firm
can it condition the development of direct understanding of realities. The intellectual understanding of the nāma or rūpa which
appears right now can only very gradually be developed. We can
come to know that the object of understanding is not a person,
a body or another concept, it is a paramattha dhamma, a nāma
or a rūpa.

The meditation subjects of samatha are concepts but they
can sometimes be paramattha dhammas such as the elements.
However, the aim is not to realize them as not self, but the
aim is to have less attachment to them. In the development of
right understanding of realities the object changes from moment
to moment, since it is the reality appearing at the present moment. One never knows what will appear next. It is different in
samatha since one has to develop calm with a meditation subject
in order to reach calm to the degree of jhāna. One may not have
the accumulated skill to develop calm to the degree of jhāna.
However, one can also develop calm in daily life, naturally, as the
occasion arises. For example, when the characteristic of mettā is
correctly known, mettā can naturally arise in daily life, without
the need to think, "I should have more mettā". Mettā can be
understood as a conditioned reality, a type of nāma which is not
self. Moments of calm and moments of right understanding can
arise naturally in daily life, but it all depends on the degree of
paññā that has been developed.

In order to have right understanding of nāma and rūpa there
should be awareness of whatever reality appears through one of
the six doors. This is very difficult and therefore you wonder
whether in the beginning it would not be better to be aware of
only what appears, for example, through the body-door. Should

one not limit the object of awareness? You find that some suttas seem to suggest this. You quote the story of Pothila from the Dhammapada commentary (282, commentary to verse 282). A novice who was an arahat instructed the monk Pothila by way of a simile. If there are six holes in an anthill and a lizard enters the anthill by one of these holes, one could catch the lizard by stopping up five of these holes, leaving the sixth one open. Then he could catch the lizard in the hole by which he entered. In the same way should Pothila deal with the six doors of the senses and the mind; he should close five of the six doors, and devote his attention to the door of the mind. We then read that he was mindful of the body and began mind development. After hearing a stanza from the Buddha he attained arahatship. It was the following stanza:

> From meditation springs wisdom,
> From lack of meditation wisdom dwindles away
> He that knows this twofold path of gain and loss
> Should so settle himself that wisdom may increase.

When wisdom has been fully developed one will not be shaken anymore by gain and loss and the other worldly conditions.

What will happen if one tells oneself that one now will concentrate on only one doorway, such as the body-door? Then there would not be understanding of the reality which appears, but there is an idea of self who sets his mind on one object, who selects the object of understanding. He thinks of it and tries to concentrate on it. While he tries to control understanding he will not know that each reality arises because of its own conditions, that it is beyond control. Some texts seem to stress understanding and mindfulness of the body, other texts emphasize understanding of feeling or other realities. Why is that? This is only to remind us not to be forgetful of the realities which appear.

When there is mindfulness and understanding of hardness which appears through the bodysense it can be known that it is only a kind of rūpa, not "my body". There is also the nāma which experiences the hardness, or the nāma which feels. If one applies oneself to the "Application of Mindfulness of the Body" it does not mean that only rūpa should be understood. If one is ignorant of nāma which appears one will continue to cling to an idea of self who experiences objects. One should know that it is only an element which experiences, not self.

When we read about the "Applications of Mindfulness" or about mindfulness in vipassanā, we should not forget that there are different levels of sati, mindfulness or awareness. Sati is a sobhana cetasika, a beautiful mental factor, that accompanies every kusala citta. It is non-forgetful of kusala. It can be of many levels. Sati of the level of dāna arises when one is generously giving gifts. Sati of the level of sīla arises when one abstains from harsh speech or when one is helping others. Sati of the level of samatha, calm, is non-forgetful of the object of calm. Sati of the level of intellectual understanding accompanies understanding of the reality appearing at the present moment, but it is not direct awareness. Sati of the level of satipaṭṭhāna is direct awareness of the reality appearing at the present moment. It accompanies paññā so that it can know this reality as only a conditioned dhamma that is not self or mine. If one does not know about these different levels one may take thinking of realities for direct awareness of the level of satipaṭṭhāna. Thus, in the context of satipaṭṭhāna and insight there are direct awareness and direct understanding of realities.

The first stage of insight is knowing the difference between the characteristic of nāma and the characteristic of rūpa. Thus, both nāma and rūpa which appear should be object of mindfulness and understanding. It depends on conditions whether there is more often mindfulness of hardness, of visible object, of feeling, or of any other reality. This is different for different people. However, we should not deliberately limit the object of mindfulness, we should not set any rule, because that is desire and this hinders the development of the eightfold Path.

Eventually all objects appearing through the six doors have to be known. Pothila could not have attained arahatship had he been ignorant of particular objects. Some people have the inclination to develop both samatha and vipassanā. In the development of samatha one subdues attachment to sense objects. However, in the development of insight there must be understanding of all nāmas and rūpas which appear so that they will be seen as only dhammas, not self. We may think that some suttas stress only one object as object of awareness, but it is important to read all texts. Then we will see that all realities should be seen as they are. We read, for example, in the "Kindred Sayings" (V, Mahā-vagga, Kindred Sayings on the Way, Ch III, § 10) that the Buddha, while he was at Sāvatthī, explained to Uttiya about the "five sensual elements". The Buddha said:

> "There are objects cognizable by the eye, objects desirable, pleasant, delightful and dear, passion-fraught, inciting to lust. There are sounds cognizable by the ear, objects desirable... there are scents cognizable by the nose... savours cognizable by the tongue... tangibles cognizable by the body, objects desirable, pleasant, delightful and dear, passion fraught, inciting to lust. These, Uttiya, are the five sensual elements of which I spoke.

> Now, Uttiya, in order to abandon these five sensual elements the ariyan eightfold way must be cultivated[2]."

---

[2]The P.T.S. translation has: it is by abandoning these five sensual elements that the ariyan eightfold way is to be cultivated, but this is not correct. I follow the Thai translation.

It is not possible to try to achieve immediately detachment from the five sense objects. Detachment can only be achieved by right understanding which realizes these objects as they are. One has to begin to be mindful of whatever object appears through one of the six doors so that understanding can gradually develop. First the clinging to self has to be eradicated and it is only at the third stage of enlightenment that attachment to sense objects is eradicated.

You asked how we can learn to discern the difference between nāma and rūpa, and in particular the difference between bodily phenomena and the experience of bodily phenomena, since that is so difficult. Is there again an idea of self who can select phenomena in order to be aware of them? We know that the difference between nāma and rūpa should be distinguished, but the objects of awareness and right understanding should not be selected. We are ignorant of all phenomena which appear. Do we know visible object as it is, seeing as it is, feeling as it is? When visible object appears it can be object of awareness so that right understanding of it can be developed. Right understanding can realize visible object as rūpa, different from nāma.

Only when the first stage of insight knowledge arises, the difference between the nāma and the rūpa which appear is clearly known; the objects of awareness are not necessarily seeing and visible object or hearing and sound. The objects of awareness are any kind of rūpa which appears and any kind of nāma which appears, there is no selection of objects, there is no idea that they would have to appear in a particular order. When we worry about it how we can know the difference between a particular kind of nāma and a particular kind of rūpa we are not developing understanding.

Why do we discuss visible object time and again? In order to be reminded to consider it with right understanding. When we see, we think immediately of the people and the things around us, because we always did this. However, we can remember that what appears through the eyes is only visible object. We need to discuss many realities, and then, if there is no selection of particular objects, there will be conditions for gradually understanding the nature of rūpa and of nāma. There is also the reality which experiences visible object. It is not self, it is only an element which experiences. We should know that enlightenment cannot be attained by developing satipaṭṭhāna only during one life-time.

We read in the "Gradual Sayings" (Book of the Threes, Ch XIV, § 131, Fighting-man) that a fighting-man has three qualities: he is a far-shooter, a shooter like lightning and a piercer of huge objects. A monk who is worthy of respect should have these three qualities. We read:

> Now, in what way is a monk a far-shooter? Herein, whatsoever rūpa... feeling... perception (saññā)... activity (saṅkhārakkhandha)... whatsoever consciousness he has, be it past, present or future, personal or external to self, be it gross or subtle, mean or exalted, far or near,- everything in short of which he is conscious,- he sees it as it really is by right insight thus: This is not mine. This am I not. This is not for me the Self. That is how a monk is "a far-shooter".

The five khandhas, all conditioned rūpas and nāmas should be realized as they are. We then read that the monk is a shooter like lightning when he understands the four noble Truths: dukkha, its origination, its ceasing and the Way leading to its ceasing. He is a piercer of huge objects when he pierces through the huge mass of ignorance.

If one wants to learn the art of shooting with bow and arrow one has to have endless patience and perseverance to learn this skill. Evenso one needs great patience and perseverance to develop satipaṭṭhāna. It has to be learnt without an idea of self who is training. The right conditions have to be there in order to be able to develop right understanding. The person who shoots from far and can hit the aim very precisely is like the person who has developed paññā which has become so keen that it can realize the true nature of the reality which appears. Paññā is as swift as lightning and it can pierce through the huge mass of ignorance. Since ignorance has been accumulated for aeons it cannot be eradicated within a short time.

With mettā,

Nina

Letter 9

Knowing ourselves

The Hague,
July 29, 1991

Do we really want to know attachment, lobha, when it appears? We know that whatever reality appears can be object of understanding but we dislike our defilements and are inclined to try to ignore them. We would rather be free from them, but we forget that the only way to eventually eliminate them is to have right understanding of them. We read in "As it was said" (Khuddaka Nikāya, Itivuttaka, The Ones, Ch I, par. 9) that the Buddha said:

> "Monks, the man who does not understand and comprehend lust, who has not detached his mind therefrom, who has not abandoned lust, can make no growth in extinguishing dukkha. But, monks, he who does understand and comprehend lust, who has detached his mind therefrom, who has abandoned lust, can make growth in extinguishing dukkha.
>
> This is the meaning of what the Exalted One said. Herein this meaning is thus spoken.

105

By whatsoever lust inflamed
Beings to the ill-bourn go,
That lust, completely knowing it,
Those who have insight do reject.
Rejecting it, no more again
They come unto this world at all.
This meaning also was spoken by the Exalted One;
   so I have heard."

The same is said about ill-will, delusion, wrath, and spite. One may believe that defilements can be abandoned without thoroughly knowing them, but this is impossible. Is there not a tendency to flee from one's defilements instead of understanding them with courage and sincerity? So long as there is ignorance our defilements are hidden, they are covered up. When we listen to the Dhamma and consider it, and when we begin to develop understanding of whatever reality appears we come to know more the defilements which were hidden to us before. We come to know our true accumulations. As we read in the sutta, they can only be eliminated by knowing them with insight. So long as they are taken for self they can never be eradicated.

Sarah sent me some tapes which were recorded in Bangkok with discussions about the development of right understanding. These discussions were held in Acharn Sujin's house and also during a trip to Kanchanaburi. Sarah said that many people want to change their character, that they want to become a better person. There is so much quarreling in daily life and people become disappointed when their life does not change for the better after they have listened to the Dhamma. They hope to be able to change themselves in a meditation center if they work very hard at it. Acharn Sujin remarked that the cittas which quarrel are anattā , not self, that they arise because of conditions. Right understanding can see that there is nobody at that moment. There is only nāma which experiences and even the words that are spoken are motivated by different mental qualities, they do not belong to anybody. Sarah said that one's aim may be a quiet, peaceful life without quarrels. However, dosa, aversion or anger, is only eradicated at the third stage of enlightenment, the stage of the "non-returner", the anāgāmī. Acharn Sujin said:

"Instead of minding too much about different defilements one could develop understanding of realities, so that all akusala will become less. Ignorance which is the cause of all akusala will be eliminated by right understanding. Maybe one is just satisfied to have less quarreling, and there is no development of understanding, no elimination of ignorance, but that depends on one's inclinations."

Several of the discussions were about going to a meditation center since many people believe that that is beneficial. They think that it is helpful to be away from people. They should find out whether that is their nature and whether it helps them to become more detached, to have less clinging. Does it help them to understand their own accumulations more deeply? Some people believe that an "intensive course" in a center can be a short-cut to reach the goal. How can there be a short-cut if there is no understanding of this moment? The understanding of this very moment should be the test for our progress. Acharn Sujin said:

"If there is understanding now it can be accumulated. One has to notice desire, whether it is there. Instead of having desire there can be awareness and right understanding even now. That is the meaning of the 'Middle Way'. Understanding realities with awareness, that is the moment of progress. You think that you can get rid of desire, somewhere, at some time, but what about this moment? There is lobha if there is no understanding. Desire is not self, it is a reality. If you don't understand it, you will not get rid of it. When you look at the newspaper you can develop understanding about lobha which is conditioned. You

cannot do anything about it, but there can be understanding of
lobha as a conditioned reality."

Different people will react differently when they hear, "you
cannot do anything about it", it all depends on the understanding of the listener. It is right understanding when we realize that
we cannot do anything about the realities which arise because of
their own conditions. In this way we shall come to understand
that they are beyond control, anattā. There is wrong understanding if one believes that it is senseless to develop kusala and
right understanding since one cannot do anything about one's
defilements. When people speak harsh words to us it is beneficial to realize that we cannot do anything about the hearing,
since it is conditioned already. Hearing is vipāka, the result of
kamma. As Acharn Sujin said, there is nobody there, there is
only the experiencing. No self hears, it is only a type of nāma,
and no self gets hurt by harsh words. When we consider this
more deeply and there can be understanding of whatever reality appears now, we shall be less inclined to retort unpleasant
words. We shall have more understanding of the truth that there
is nobody there.

Acharn Sujin explained:

"The idea of self always pushes one this or that way. The
development of understanding just follows all realities. Then
lobha cannot push you to cover up the realities which have arisen
now because of conditions. Just understand any reality which is
conditioned. Seeing now is conditioned and therefore it arises,
it sees. Develop understanding of the reality which is already
conditioned."

Jonothan remarked that one may have regret about losing
opportunities for the study of Dhamma, about not having considered the Dhamma more often. Acharn Sujin remarked:

"While talking about realities the 'perfection' of paññā develops by itself, even if we do not name it or talk about the
resolution to develop the perfections. You would not have come

from Hong Kong to have discussions if you did not have the determination to develop paññā. Your action shows it. Any moment can be a moment of developing the perfections. Listening is not always convenient, but one can still develop perfections when there is no opportunity for listening or studying."

We may have regret about our lack of study and we may wonder whether we should avoid particular situations like going out and enjoying ourselves, in order to have more time for study and for consideration of the Dhamma. There is still the idea of self which pushes us this way or that way. Instead, we should just "follow" all realities which appear.

Alan Weller wrote a letter to me about this subject and I quote:

"I used to think that I should study the Dhamma and be alone rather than going out with friends. It seems as if there is no self indulgence when we do not go to the movies whereas in actual fact defilements are around all the time. The stories on the screen are no different from the stories in our everyday life. We have pleasant feeling or unpleasant feeling conditioned by what we see, no matter whether we are at the movies or not. All situations are the same in the sense that they consist of realities which are anicca (impermanent), dukkha (unsatisfactory), and anattā (non-self). Pleasant feeling has its own characteristic which can be understood, no matter where we are. We cannot force kusala by listening more to the Dhamma. Akusala is conditioned by accumulation, we have to accept it as it is. By listening to the Dhamma and considering it there are conditions for the development of kusala, slowly and gradually.

We should follow our own accumulations wisely, sincerely, understanding them as they really are. I have accumulations to go to the movies, watch T.V. and read magazines. The interest in these is a conditioned reality which can be known. Also the interest in Dhamma is conditioned. I cannot force myself to have more interest in the Dhamma. I understand the value of reading the scriptures and considering the Dhamma and that is a condition for studying it. We cannot read all day, every day. Therefore it is best to live our life naturally according to our own accumulation and to learn to apply Dhamma in any situation.

Whenever we study the Dhamma there is renunciation, so of course sometimes we shall study rather than watch T.V., but are we doing this because of renunciation or because of desire? There can so easily be attachment. This should be seen as it is, otherwise our studying will be overmuch, too tense, not according to our own real nature. We should not force ourselves to have more kusala by being in a particular situation.

To sum up: any time is Dhamma time, but reading, listening to tapes, asking questions is valuable. We have to balance our own accumulation with the study of Dhamma. Too much going to the movies and we shall neglect reading and considering. Too much reading and considering may be forced and too tense. We should be easy going, learning to see dhamma as dhamma and realizing the danger of too much self indulgence. Attachment is constantly moving us away from Dhamma."

The perfection of truthfulness or sincerity is indispensable for the development of paññā. Susie wrote to me that she realized that there are, after seeing, many moments of thinking of stories about people and things. She wrote:

"I certainly see that I get so absorbed that I don't want to hear, read or think about Dhamma. I would rather have my lobha and my story. Pretty natural."

This is sincere. If we try to force ourselves not to be absorbed in stories about people and things there is already desire for result. There is the idea of self who is "doing something" and then we are on the wrong path. Only if we naturally follow all realities, also the moments of being absorbed, we are on the "Middle Way", and then understanding can develop. Do we mind what kind of reality arises? Do we mind lack of sati? We may think that we do not mind but as understanding develops, one knows that one minds a lot. How much or how little we mind indicates to what extent understanding has developed. We can only find out ourselves. When understanding has developed more it does not matter at all which type of reality appears since all realities that arise are conditioned.

Jonothan remarked that he is just as happy to know dosa as to know generosity, because in the end all realities have to be known as they are. It is very beneficial to be reminded that we should find out how much we mind about the realities which appear. It teaches us to become more sincere. Without noticing it we may have preference for particular realities and we may forgetful of certain other realities. We may want to know seeing but we are unhappy about the thinking which arises on account of what we saw, and, thus, we may ignore that reality. We dislike dosa, and, thus, we may not want to know that reality when it appears. Acharn Sujin said:

"One can benefit from having lobha or dosa. One can see to what extent one has accumulated these realities. Isn't it useful? One can see one's akusala. Otherwise one could not know how much one has. No one likes it, but instead of disliking it why not use it as an opportunity for the development of understanding. It is very beneficial to understand akusala in detail. It always arises and it is there, from morning to night, but it is not understood as such. Paññā can see akusala as a conditioned nāma, so that the idea of self will be eliminated from all akusala of all levels. If there is no understanding of akusala how can one know whether one has less akusala or more? If there is no understanding of akusala can one say that one has developed understanding?"

Many conditions are necessary for the arising of direct understanding, such as reading, discussing and considering the characteristic of whatever reality appears at the present moment. When we remember that intellectual understanding of the present reality, pariyatti, must be firm, we shall be less inclined to induce direct awareness and understanding. There is awareness, sati, accompanying intellectual understanding, but it is different from direct awareness of realities. If one tries hard to make direct awareness arise one thinks that there is awareness, but it is not right awareness. We may mistakenly think that there is direct awareness of realities when we are only thinking about realities such as softness or the experience of softness.

In some meditation centers people have to sit for one hour, then walk for one hour, but there is no right understanding of the present reality. They may hear the teacher say that softness is rūpa and that the experience of softness is not self. They learn by heart that there are six doorways and they recite for themselves the objects which can appear through these doorways. This can be a level of sati since sati accompanies each kind of kusala citta, but there is no development of direct understanding of the reality appearing at the present moment. When paññā is being developed there will be less doubt about the realities that appear. One shall be less inclined to think, "Was there direct awareness of realities or was it only thinking?"

People want to know what the characteristic of visible object is, and Acharn Sujin gave a very meaningful explanation which is well worth considering:

"A reality. Can anybody do something about it at this moment? It appears now, it has its own characteristic, nobody can change it."

Visible object is just a reality, it is not a person or a tree, as we used to think. When we hear that it is a reality and that we cannot do anything about it, it reminds us of the nature of anattā of visible object. It appears already and understanding of it can be naturally developed. It seems that we see immediately a chair or a flower, but if there were no thinking could there be any idea about visible object? Seeing and thinking arise closely one after the other and gradually their different characteristics can be known.

Someone remarked that it is a relief to understand kamma

and vipāka[1], to know that things have to happen and that it is of no use to try to control one's life.

When one thinks, "It is kamma, it is vipāka", it is only thinking and not understanding of realities. We say that seeing and hearing are vipāka, but we just repeat what is in the text. Our understanding is still superficial. As paññā develops it will see more clearly what kamma is and what vipāka and it will realize them as non-self.

While one is developing understanding one should not expect clear understanding of realities immediately. Acharn Sujin remarked that the sharp and keen understanding is the result which will arise later, one should not have expectations. One is on the right way and one does not mind when and where there will be result, it will arise when it is the right time. There can be understanding of seeing right now, one does not have to waste time.

When right understanding is developed in daily life it can condition more patience in the different situations. Situations change all the time and life can be complicated. We may be overburdened by work or we may have problems concerning our relatives. I will quote a conversation about the perfection of patience between Acharn Sujin and Sarah.

Acharn: "If there are no difficult situations how does one know that right understanding can cope with them, that it can know the different realities which appear? When there is more understanding of realities as not self there is more patience. When there is patience it can be understood as 'nobody'."

Sarah: "Is there more patience because one tries less to control realities?"

Acharn: "There is less attachment to self."

Sarah: "Will there be less frustration about situations?"

---

[1]Kamma, a good or bad deed committed in the past, that produces its appropriate result, vipāka, in the form of rebirth or in the form of pleasant or unpleasant sense-cognitions.

Acharn: "And also less disturbance while one thinks about other people. One understands that there is no permanent being. Sound arises and falls away, it does not belong to any one. When people speak the sound is conditioned by the nāma-kkhandhas and these also fall away. There is only the thinking of a story about people and things all the time. It is the same as when we watch T.V., read the newspaper or dream about things. What is seen is only visible object. When there is patience one is not disturbed by any circumstances.

One may be inclined to think of a self who cannot bear anymore such or such situation. Patience is a condition not to have aversion. We have to cope with many situations. The growth of the perfections must be in daily life, in any situation."

Sarah: "I do not quite understand the perfection of determination or resolution, it seems that it is just thinking."

Acharn: "Thinking and taking action."

Sarah: "Following the kusala way?"

Acharn: "When I go to the Bovornives Temple to give lectures or I am preparing the tapes for the radio I do not have to think about which perfections I am developing. The action shows the perfections.

It is not self but sankhārakkhandha (the khandha of 'activities' or 'formations') which conditions the thinking, 'I will do as much kusala as possible', and also the action in accordance with the thinking. Resolution is not only thinking. One needs the perfection of sincerity or truthfulness in order to conform one's deeds and speech with one's thinking to perform kusala. For example, you have the intention to have right speech but when the situation arises for right speech it depends on whether you have sincerity to act according to your resolution. Sincerity can condition kusala at such a moment. Then you develop kusala not for fame, admiration and other selfish motives."

When we notice the unwholesomeness of someone else we find it difficult to have kusala citta. The person who has no understanding about kusala and akusala can be object of mettā. When he commits ill deeds he does not know that it is akusala. We can have mettā instead of dosa. Then we do not follow the opinion of others who dislike such a person. When we have aversion about someone's bad deeds we accumulate more akusala.

Acharn Sujin had reminded us in India to become like a dustrag which serves for wiping the feet. A dustrag takes up filth and is undisturbed by it. One should become as humble as a dustrag. Sāriputta, who could forgive anybody, no matter whether that person treated him in an unjust manner, compared himself to a dustrag. He had no conceit. When right understanding has been developed one will cling less to the self, there will be more humbleness. During the discussions Acharn Sujin said again:

"I would like to be a dustrag. I follow the way to be one, it is my resolution. Our resolution means that we take action by developing understanding and mettā."

It is beneficial to be reminded again of the dustrag, because humbleness seems to go against our nature. As understanding develops it must lead to letting go of nāmas and rūpas. What we take for self are only impermanent nāmas and rūpas. When their impermanence has been realized can they be as important as before?

We read in the "Vinaya" (VI, Parivāra, Ch XII, The Lesser Collection, 163) how the monk should behave while approaching the Sangha when it is convened for the investigation of a legal question. We read:

> ... he should approach the Order with a humble mind, with a mind as though it were removing dust. He should be skilled about seats and skilled about sitting down. He should sit down on a suitable seat without encroaching on (the space intended for) monks who are Elders and without keeping newly ordained monks from a seat. He should not talk in a desultory

> fashion, nor about inferior (worldly) matters. Either
> he should speak Dhamma himself or should ask an-
> other to do so, or he should not disdain the ariyan
> silence ...

The commentary (the Samantapāsādika) adds to "with a
mind as though it were removing dust": "like a towel for wiping
the feet." The Vinaya contains many useful reminders about
behaviour which laypeople can apply too in their own situation.
Some people believe that when they do not harm or hurt others
by bad deeds such as killing or stealing, they have good sīla, but
actually, akusala cittas arise time and again after seeing, hearing and the other sense-cognitions. If the reality that appears
now is not clearly understood as only a conditioned dhamma
the difference between kusala citta and akusala citta cannot be
clearly known. We can only think about them. Further on in
this section of the Vinaya we read:

> ... he should not speak waving his arms about, he
> should be unhastening, he should be considerate, he
> should not be quick tempered, with a mind of loving
> kindness he should be gentle in speech; merciful, he
> should be compassionate for welfare; seeking for wel-
> fare, he should not be frivolous in speech; limiting
> his speech, he should be one who masters hostility,
> and is without irascibility.

If we want to become like a dustrag all love of self and conceit must eventually be eradicated. Right understanding should
be developed while we are busy, while we are in the company of
others. Akusala cittas are bound to arise in our dealings with
others and also when we are alone, but when akusala citta appears we have the opportunity to understand it as a conditioned
reality that is non-self.

It is helpful to be reminded that there are so many realities
we are still ignorant of. All realities which appear have to be

known in order to eliminate the idea of self. It takes more than a lifetime, as Acharn Sujin often said.

Letter 10

All realities are dukkha

The Hague,
Oct. 2, 1991

Our daily life is complicated, we are busy with our work and there are always problems which disturb us. It seems that there is very little opportunity for wholesome deeds. We believe that we see the value of the Dhamma, but we find it hard to develop understanding of realities. We read in the "Gradual Sayings" (I, Book of the Threes, Ch VI, The Brāhmins, par. 51, Two people):

> Now two broken-down old brāhmins, aged, far gone in years, who had reached life's end, one hundred and twenty years of age, came to see the Exalted One ... As they sat at one side those brāhmins said this to the Exalted One:
>
> "We are brāhmins, master Gotama, old brāhmins, aged, far gone in years ... but we have done no noble deeds, no meritorious deeds, no deeds that can bring assurance to our fears. Let the worthy Gotama cheer

us! Let the worthy Gotama comfort us, so that it
may be a profit and a blessing to us for a long time!"

"Indeed, you brāhmins are old ... but you have done
no deeds that can bring assurance to your fears. Indeed, brāhmins, this world is swept onward by old
age, by sickness, by death. Since this is so, self-
restraint in body, speech and thought (practised) in
this life:- let this be refuge, cave of shelter, island of
defense, resting-place and support for him who has
gone beyond.

Life is swept onward: brief our span of years.
One swept away by old age has no defence.
Then keep the fear of death before your eyes,
And do good deeds that lead to happiness.

The self-restraint of body, speech and thought
In this life practised, meritorious deeds,
these make for happiness when one has died."

These two brāhmins were sincere, they realized that there are
most of the time akusala cittas. Is it not the same for us? There
are more often akusala cittas than kusala cittas after seeing,
hearing, smelling, tasting or the experience of tangible object.
We are attached to all the sense objects; attachment, lobha, is
following us like a shadow throughout our lives. If the object
which is experienced is unpleasant our attachment conditions
aversion, dosa.

Acharn Sujin spoke about the sutta on the two old brāhmins
in the Bovornives Temple, explaining that it deals with our daily
life. I would like to quote her explanation:

"Conditions are different for different people. Some people
think of themselves all the time, they do not do anything for
their relatives or friends. From morning until night they are

busy with their work, making a living for their family, and they have to face many problems with regard to their duties. If one does not accumulate kusala so that it becomes one's nature, kusala citta will not arise very easily. One should accumulate kusala when one is in the company of other people, while one is working or while one has free time, otherwise there may not be any opportunity for kusala. When one takes a rest after a busy day there is likely to be lobha. One clings to self, one looks for pleasure, for distraction. Then one thinks that there is no time for kusala.

The two old brāhmins had faced many problems concerning their families. However, this is the case with all of us. We are bound to have moments that we are worried and disturbed. All kinds of problems arise every day. If there are no problems concerning our house, our family, or our work, there are numerous other occasions for worry. We are worried in this life, but we should remember that there was also worry in former lives. These worries belong to the past. Evenso the worry in this life cannot stay. There was worry in the past and there will also be worry in future lives. One worries about sickness and pain. Also in former lives there was worry about sickness, although we do not know from which diseases we were suffering. In this life we may have the same diseases or other ones we did not have before, but there is worry just as there was in past lives during the cycle of birth and death, and there will be worry again in lives to come.

We should not forget to consider again and again eight 'grounds for a sense of urgency' (Vis. IV, 63): birth, ageing, sickness and death, the sufferings connected with unhappy rebirth, the suffering in the past rooted in the cycle of rebirths, the suffering in the future rooted in the cycle of rebirths, and the suffering in the present rooted in the search for nutriment.

We cannot remember the sufferings of the past but they are not different from those arising in the present life, and also those in the future will not be different. If one has a house one is bound to worry about it again and again. If one has duties concerning one's daily work one is bound to worry again and again. Since we have a body we shall worry again and again about our health. We should ponder over the truth concerning the suffering in this life connected with the search for nutriment. We are actually searching food for dukkha. That is why we are continuously going around in the cycle, always travelling, time and again searching food for dukkha.

Whenever we experience a pleasant object through the eyes we continue to search food for dukkha. We search as it were for dukkha in the cycle of birth and death. Whenever there is hearing and we are attached to sound we are already searching for dukkha. Attachment is the cause of dukkha in the cycle. We never stop searching for dukkha. Through the nose we smell fragrant odours, the scent of flowers, of perfumes, and then we keep on searching for dukkha all around, everywhere. We search for dukkha when we taste flavour through the tongue, or when we experience tangible object through the bodysense. When we think of different subjects don't we search for dukkha? We are searching for dukkha everywhere from morning until night. If we don't realize this we cannot be freed from the cycle of birth and death.

Before defilements can be eradicated, before detachment, alobha, can arise and become powerful, so that selfishness can be given up, we should know the characteristic of the cause of dukkha, the food for dukkha. This is lobha, attachment, which searches all around. Lobha is the cause of dukkha whereas alobha, detachment, is the cause of happiness. When one has less attachment to the objects which appear through the six doors is there not less searching for dukkha? The next life will be again like this life and the cycle will be very long if paññā does not know the characteristics of realities as they are. Paññā should be developed to the degree that it realizes the four noble

Truths and enlightenment is attained.

In the next life there will be happiness and sorrow, and this depends on kamma. If one has right understanding about kamma and one has determination for kusala one will not be negligent." These were Acharn Sujin's words.

The sutta on the two old brāhmins is followed by another sutta which is partly similar. The Buddha said to the two old brāhmins that the world is all ablaze with old age, sickness and death. We then read that he spoke the following verse:

> When a house is burning, goods removed therefrom,
> Not which are burned, will be of use to him
> who removes them. So the world is burned
> By old age and death. Then save yourself by giving.
> What is given is well saved.
> The self-restraint of body, speech and mind
> In this life practised, meritorious deeds,
> These make for happiness when one has died.

Through the development of right understanding of nāma and rūpa we shall see the danger of akusala and the benefit of kusala. We shall come to see the disadvantages of being born again and again. At this moment we do not see that life is dukkha. We are searching for dukkha so long as we are attached to nāma and rūpa. We can develop more understanding of the dukkha in our life by considering what the scriptures and the commentaries state about this subject and by developing understanding of the reality appearing at this moment. We should not forget that whatever text we read points to the development of understanding at this moment. This is always implied, even if it is not directly expressed in words.

We read in the sutta quoted above about the self-restraint of body, speech and mind that make for happiness, and this points to the development of understanding of whatever object appears through one of the sense-doors or the mind-door. We usually cling to all sense objects and we keep on being attached to people and things we believe that exist. But in seeing them as they are, as only dhammas, there are conditions for reacting wisely to our experiences instead of being overwhelmed by akusala cittas. The commentary to the "Book of Analysis" (Vibhaṅga), the "Dispeller of Delusion", "Sammohavinodanī", elaborates on the different aspects of dukkha[1]. We read in the section on the "Classification of the Truths" (Ch IV, Saccavibhaṅga) about the many kinds of dukkha. We read about dukkha, suffering (93):

> Herein, bodily and mental painful feeling are called "suffering as suffering" (dukkha-dukkha, intrinsic suffering), because of their individual essence, because of their name and because of painfulness. Bodily and mental pleasant feeling are called "suffering in change" (vipariṇāma-dukkha) because of being the cause of the arising of pain through their change. Indifferent feeling and the remaining formations of the three planes are called "suffering in formations" (saṅkhāra-dukkha) because of their being oppressed by rise and fall . . .

Saṅkhāra dhammas, conditioned dhammas, which arise and fall away cannot be a refuge, thus they are dukkha. Seeing that appears now is a conditioned dhamma, it arises and falls away, it is dukkha. And this is true for all conditioned realities of our daily life.

Under the section about birth we read that birth is dukkha. The commentary explains that birth is suffering since it is the basis for the arising of suffering. Birth is the foundation of many kinds of dukkha when it occurs in the unhappy planes, and it also is the foundation of dukkha in happy planes. In the human plane there is suffering rooted in the descent into the womb. The

---

[1] See also Visuddhimagga XVI, 32-61.

commentary describes the suffering of the unborn being because of heat of the mother's body, because of cold when his mother drinks cold water, because of all the pains when his mother gives birth. In the course of an existence there is pain in one who kills himself, who practises self-torture, who through anger does not eat or who hangs himself, or who undergoes suffering through the violence of others.

Old age is dukkha. The commentary explains that it is called suffering as being the basis for both bodily and mental suffering. We read:

> ... For the person of one who is aged, is weak like an aged cart. Great suffering arises in one struggling to stand or to walk or to sit; grief arises in one when his wife and children are not as considerate as before. Thus it should be understood as suffering through being the basis for these two kinds of suffering. Furthermore:

> With leadenness in all one's limbs,
> With all one's faculties declining,
> With vanishing of youthfulness,
> With undermining of one's strength,
> With loss of memory and so on,
> With growing unattractiveness
> To one's own wife and family,
> And then with dotage coming on,
> The pain that mortals undergo,
> Alike of body and of mind-
> Since ageing causes all of this,
> Old age is thus called suffering.

Death is dukkha. The dying moment is only one moment of citta which falls away and then there is another life, but one is no longer the same person. Death is called suffering because it is the basis for both mental and bodily suffering. There is bodily suffering before dying and also mental suffering. When one loses one's possessions one is unhappy, but at death one loses everything, one loses one's body, one loses one's life as this particular person. Death is the greatest dukkha. We are attached to our possessions and we may be inclined to stinginess. If we remember that at death we have to leave everything behind it can be a condition for being less stingy. Stinginess can condition akusala kamma leading to an unhappy rebirth. "If we want to save things for ourselves we actually save them for Hell", Acharn Sujin explained. The commentary states that those who, because of akusala kamma, are destined for an unhappy rebirth, have great fear and grief shortly before dying. At that moment the akusala kamma they committed or an image of Hell can appear to them. Thus we see that death is the basis for bodily and mental suffering.

Sorrow (soka) is dukkha. Sorrow ruins, it rejects and destroys welfare, the commentary states. There are five kinds of ruins or losses: of relatives, of property, of health, of virtue, sīla, and of right view. When one is affected by one of these losses and one is overwhelmed by it one has sorrow. These ruins are part of our daily life. One may lose relatives when robbers kill them, or one may lose them because of a war or because of disease. It is obvious that loss of relatives, of property and of health causes sorrow. As to loss of sīla, this can cause one to worry about it and to suffer greatly. When there is loss of right view, one has wrong view, and this can condition many kinds of bad deeds which will bring unpleasant results. So long as one is attached to wrong view there is no way to become free from the cycle of birth and death. The commentary uses the words "inner sorrow" and "heart-burning". We read: " ... for sorrow when it arises burns, consumes the mind like fire and makes one say: 'My mind is on fire. I cannot think of anything.' " Sorrow is compared to a dart which causes pain. It is the basis for both bodily and mental suffering. We read in the commentary that it has the characteristic of inner consuming, that its nature is to completely consume the mind and that its manifestation is continual sorrowing. We read the following verse:

> Sorrow like a (poisoned) arrow
> penetrates the heart of beings,
> And like a spear hot from the fire
> most grievously it keeps on burning.
> And since it brings on many kinds
> of suffering such as disease,
> Old age and death, this too has thus
> acquired the name of suffering.

In the "Gradual Sayings" (Book of the Twos, Ch I, no. 3, Tapanīyā Sutta) we read about the burning of remorse:

> Monks, there are these two things that sear (the conscience). What two? Herein, a certain one has done an immoral act of body, he has done immoral acts in speech and thought, has omitted moral acts in body, speech and thought. He is seared (with remorse) at the thought: I have done wrong in body, speech and thought. I have left undone the good deed in body, speech and thought. And he burns at the thought of it. These, monks, are the two things that sear (the conscience).

The commentary to this sutta, the "Manorathapūranī", illustrates how a bad conscience can cause great sorrow. We read that two brothers killed a cow and divided the flesh. However, the younger brother wanted to have more since he had many children. They had a fight and then the older brother killed the younger one. He realized that he had committed grave akusala kamma and kept on worrying about it. He could find no rest, no matter he was standing or sitting and he could no longer digest his food, so that he finally became only skin and bone. He was afterwards reborn in Hell as a result of his akusala kamma.

Lamentation (parideva) is dukkha. It is the basis for both bodily and mental suffering. We read:

> Struck by sorrow's dart a man laments,
> Yet thus makes worse the pain born of dry throat
> And lips and palate, and unbearable-
> So the Blessed One called lamentation pain.

Pain is dukkha. Both bodily and mental pain are dukkha, because each of these is the basis for both bodily and mental suffering. When one is afflicted by bodily pain one also suffers mentally. When one is over-whelmed by grief one may bring bodily pain upon oneself by thumping one's breast or even by committing suicide.

Woe (upāyāsa) is dukkha because it is also the basis for bodily and mental suffering. According to the commentary, it has the characteristic of frustration, its nature is moaning and it manifests itself as dejection.

Furthermore, the commentary elaborates on the kinds of dukkha which are: association with the undesired, separation from the desired and not getting what one wishes. These are also the basis for both bodily and mental suffering.

The five khandhas of clinging in short are dukkha. The commentary explains:

> In the description of the khandhas as objects of cling-
> ing, "in short" (sankhittena) is said with reference
> to the manner of teaching. For suffering cannot be
> summed up in short as so many hundred kinds of
> suffering, or so many thousand kinds of suffering, or
> so many hundred thousand kinds of suffering; but it
> can by the manner of teaching. Therefore he spoke

thus, summing up the teaching in short in this way:
"There is no other suffering at all, but in short the
five khandhas as objects of clinging are suffering."

According to the commentary the different kinds of suffering
are generated in the five khandhas as grass is on the ground or
fruits and flowers are on trees. Dukkha is inherent in the five
khandhas of clinging.

The fact that, in short, the five khandhas of clinging are
dukkha reminds us of the ultimate truth. There is no being in
the ultimate sense, there are only the five khandhas, nāma and
rūpa. They arise and then fall away immediately and thus they
are unsatisfactory, one cannot take one's refuge in them. We
may say that there is nothing desirable in life, that life is dukkha,
but have we realized the truth of dukkha? Right understanding
of the reality appearing at this moment should be developed,
because this is the only way to know the truth about nāma and
rūpa.

We usually react with akusala citta when we experience pleasant and unpleasant objects. We are disturbed by the eight
"worldly conditions" of gain and loss, praise and blame, honour
and dishonour, bodily well-being and misery. It is kamma which
is the cause of our birth and which produces the sense organs
through which we experience pleasant and unpleasant objects.
Seeing, hearing and the other sense-impressions are results of
kamma. If it were not for kamma there could not be seeing,
hearing or the experience of tangible object at this moment. We
cannot see the deeds committed in the past which produce results now but we should remember that we are heirs to kamma.
We keep on clinging to the "self" and we wonder why this or
that unpleasant experience had to happen to "me". We usually
forget that whatever happens has to happen because of conditions. When we suffer a loss there are sorrow, lamentation and
woe, we complain and we are sorry for ourselves. When such

moments arise there can be understanding of whatever occurs as only a conditioned reality.

When paññā of the degree of pariyatti, intellectual understanding, has developed to the degree that the first stage of insight can arise nāma is known as nāma and rūpa as rūpa, their different characteristics are clearly distinguished. This stage can only be reached when understanding has been developed of all kinds of nāma and rūpa which appear at the present moment through the six doors. When a stage of isight arises there is no self, no world, there are only nāma and rūpa which are conditioned. With each stage of insight there is also a growth of understanding of kamma and its result. Instead of reacting to the worldly conditions with akusala citta there will be more conditions to react wisely. Eventually there can be more patience and equanimity towards the adversities of life.

Letter 11

See Dhamma as Dhamma

We read in the "Kindred Sayings" (I, Sagāthā-vagga, Ch I, The Devas, 3, The Sword Suttas, § 1, By impending Sword) that a deva said to the Buddha:

> As one downsmitten by impending sword,
> As one whose hair and turban are aflame,
> So let the bhikkhu, mindful and alert,
> Go forth, all worldly passions left behind.

The Exalted One said:

> As one downsmitten by impending sword,
> As one whose hair and turban are aflame,
> So let the bhikkhu, mindful and alert,
> Go forth, leaving personality-belief behind.

Just as the person who has been struck by a sword or whose hair and turban are aflame will not be neglectful but apply energy to overcome his dangerous situation, evenso should the bhikkhu not be neglectful, but develop right understanding of realities that appear now. The Buddha repeated what the deva

said, but he changed one sentence, and this change is very meaningful. The deva spoke about subduing the sense pleasures, but
so long as they have not been eradicated, will one be bound
by clinging to them. They cannot be eradicated when there is
still the wrong view of self. We read in the commentary to this
sutta, the "Sāratthappakāsinī", that the Buddha, in view of this,
wanted to change the deva's verse, using the same similes but ap-
plying them to the magga-citta of the sotāpanna (the streamwinner, who attains the first stage of enlightenment), which citta
eradicates personality-belief, sakkāya diṭṭhi.

We may easily overlook the subtle point of this sutta. We
understand in theory that first of all wrong view has to be eradicated before finally, at the third stage of enlightenment, the
stage of the anāgāmī (non-returner), clinging to sense pleasures
can be eradicated. Even though we know this, we are still inclined to worry about our attachment to sense pleasures instead
of knowing its characteristic when it appears. This is the only
way to finally be able to eradicate it.

"Should we hate our akusala? It is just a reality, it arises",
Acharn Sujin reminded Sarah and Jonothan while they were in
Bangkok. They recorded their conversations with Acharn Sujin
and I shall give an account of the contents of them. Acharn Sujin
explained that she does not think that she should get rid of all
defilements now. She remarked:

"I do not think, 'defilements are so ugly', they are just realities. There should be understanding of them. People want
to get rid of all defilements but they do not have any understanding of them. Why should our first objective not be right
understanding? I do not understand why people are so much irritated by their defilements. One is drawn to the idea of self all
the time, while one thinks about it whether one has less defilements or more. There is no understanding but merely thinking
of kusala and akusala as 'ours'. So long as there is ignorance
there must be different degrees of akusala. We should just de-

velop understanding of whatever reality appears. At the moment of developing understanding one is not carried away by thoughts about the amount of one's defilements, wondering about it how many defilements one has or whether they are decreasing."

We may not notice that we think of kusala and akusala as "ours", but the idea is there. Acharn Sujin's reminders can help us to consider more thoroughly what motivates our actions, speech and thoughts. Is it not mostly clinging to ourselves? Some people, when they reflect on lobha, have dosa, displeasure about it. Acharn Sujin remarked:

"That is only reflection, not the understanding of the characteristic which is not self. Who could change the characteristic of attachment. Understanding should be developed in a natural way. This is a relief. Even if lobha arises again, we should realize it as only a reality. You can understand the characteristic of lobha we talk about a great deal. It's nature is non-self. This way of developing understanding is the most effective way. Then there is no attachment or aversion towards the object which appears. You should not stop pleasure, it is not 'you'."

The object which appears is the object of which understanding should be developed. When understanding is being developed there is no attachment nor dislike of the object; no attachment when the object is kusala, no dislike when the object is akusala. We do not have to feel guilty when we enjoy ourselves, the enjoyment is only a reality. When we think of our defilements it is actually thinking of ourselves in a particular way all the time. Did we notice how busy we are with "ourselves"?

When we have problems in our daily life we become frustrated and we find it difficult to have understanding of whatever appears now. Acharn Sujin said:

"When there is no awareness there has not been enough listening and not enough intellectual understanding of the objects of insight. One may think that it is enough to know that there are nāma and rūpa, but their characteristics have to be realized.

Knowing the details of realities can help one to see their nature of anattā. This is very important for the growth of paññā. One has to become 'a person who has listened a lot', in Pāli: bahussutta, in order to attain enlightenment."

Sarah asked Acharn Sujin questions about the object of right understanding and about details one has to know. I shall quote from their conversation occurring during a traffic jam in Bangkok which lasted for hours:

Acharn: "One has to know the details of each of the six doorways, of the way realities are conditioned, of realities as dhātus, elements, of the āyatanas, bases or sense-fields[1]. The Buddha taught for fortyfive years about nāma and rūpa. Sāriputta understood as soon as he heard the word 'dhamma', he understood realities as nāma and rūpa. For us it is different, we have to listen again and again and to consider what nāma is and what rūpa is. Seeing right now is an experience, it is just a reality. One has to consider and listen and discuss a great deal about these subjects."

Sarah: "We have considered seeing and discussed about the details of realities a great deal, I wonder how much more we should hear about it."

Acharn: "Until awareness is aware with understanding right now. That is why the Buddha taught for fortyfive years about nāma and rūpa. The Abhidhamma is the essence of his teachings. He taught about paramattha dhammas so that one can see the difference between paramattha dhammas and concepts. He taught the conditions for realities. Knowing which cetasikas accompany citta helps one to see the nature of anattā. It is amazing that there are so many conditions needed for one moment of experiencing visible object, and then that moment is gone com-

---

[1]The five senses, the five sense objects, citta and objects experienced through the mind-door, namely, subtle rūpa, cetasikas and nibbāna, have been classified as āyatanas.

pletely. It is all very intricate, not everyone can understand this instantly."

Sarah: "It is never is enough, one can always know the object more precisely and in a more detailed way."

Acharn: "Otherwise we underestimate the Buddha's wisdom, we may think that he used just common, ordinary words. He taught us, so that by listening and considering more and more we could one day become a sotāpanna[2]. By gradually developing understanding we can acquire full understanding of realities which appear. Right understanding of visible object and seeing is the only way to eradicate the latent tendencies of 'I see', and 'me', which are there all the time. Whenever there is feeling, it is 'me' again. The Buddha taught about five khandhas[3], he taught in many different ways in order to help people to consider more, to understand more, so that, when there is awareness, right understanding can gradually develop."

People become impatient when there is not direct awareness and understanding of seeing, visible object, sound and other realities that appear. They do not realize that intellectual understanding of the reality appearing now should be firm. Only then will there be conditions for satipaṭṭhāna or the direct awareness and understanding of the reality that appears.

As Acharn often emphasized, the perfections, pāramīs, should be accumulated. The Buddha, when he was a Bodhisatta, developed these for aeons so that he would attain Buddhahood in his last life. Evenso do we need to develop the perfections so that

---

[2]There are four stages of enlightenment: the stage of the sotāpanna (streamwinner), the sakadāgāmī (once-returner), the anāgāmī (non-returner) and the arahat, the perfected one. At each stage defilements are progressively eradicated until they are all eradicated at the attainment of arahatship.

[3]Conditioned realities are classified as five khandhas or aggregates: the khandha of rūpa, physical phenomena, of vedanā, feeling, of saññā, perception or memory, saṅkhāra-khandha, mental factors or cetasikas, except feeling and perception, and viññāṇa, consciousness.

enlightenment can be attained. Acharn said:

"All pāramīs are needed. We should not be careless about them and we should not neglect any one of them. Paññā is needed above all, the other nine pāramīs are the "attendants" of paññā. Without paññā the other pāramīs cannot develop."

We read in the commentary to the "Cariyāpiṭaka", the "Paramatthadīpanī", that the aspiration (to become a Buddha) and also great compassion and skilful means are conditions for the pāramīs. We read:

"Therein, skilful means is the wisdom which transforms dāna (and the other nine virtues) into requisites for enlightenment."

At the moment there is right understanding of realities there is no clinging to "my kusala". However, we usually cling, we want to be "a good person". We find that it feels better to have kusala citta, and then there is clinging again. When we observe the five precepts or eight precepts, there is likely to be clinging; do we want to be better than others who do not observe precepts? When we think of the development of mettā, we may be wondering how much mettā we have already, we may try to "measure" it. Then we are again thinking of "my kusala", instead of developing mettā. We should not underestimate the accumulation of defilements. We do not notice the lobha that clings to "self", that wants the "self" to be good. Acharn Sujin remarked that when there is no understanding there is lobha.

When we try to have mettā instead of anger, is there clinging to "self"? When someone is about to lose his temper he may try to be patient. It is unpleasant for the people around oneself if one gives in to anger. We may see that anger is useless and then sati can arise which prevents the arising of anger. There is no "self " who tries, but sati which performs its function. This is one level of sati but it is not sati of satipaṭṭhāna accompanying paññā which sees realities as nāma and rūpa, not self. When there is wrong view of self who tries to stop anger it will not be effective. Acharn Sujin remarked:

"One should not cling to the idea of 'I have lots of anger, I try not to have it.' Then there is only thinking with the idea of self all the time. I don't mind what level of akusala will arise, even if it is strong anger. It arises and then it is gone, it cannot stay. What about the present moment? I always encourage people to have right understanding instead of trying to control with the idea of self. If that is the case they will never reach the level of understanding realities, not even understanding based on reflection about nāma and rūpa. There can be awareness of anger. When it arises and performs its function it is there to see its characteristic as 'just a reality', instead of thinking about it."

People are wondering whether it would not be useful sometimes to set rules for one's behaviour. One may wonder how one can correct unwholesome speech.

Acharn Sujin remarked that whatever one is doing or not doing, it is not self. Don't we forget that all the time? We know that we have not eradicated the clinging to the idea of "self", but we do not realize how deeply rooted wrong view is. Acharn Sujin said:

"Even when one wants to set rules there is no self, it is only thinking. The only way to get rid of the self is to understand all situations. One should not set any rules, there should only be development of understanding of realities. Unwholesome speech can be corrected by paññā which sees its danger and that is one level of sati. Another level is sati of satipaṭṭhāna. The most precious moment is the moment of being aware. If one forces oneself, sets rules or clings to a certain practice it does not help one to understand this moment, one's thinking, seeing or hearing."

Instead of being aware of this moment we are carried away by our thinking of stories about other people or events which took place. We think of other people's lobha, dosa and moha and this conditions aversion. We cannot change someone else because each moment is conditioned. If there can be understanding of our own akusala which arises, the object is a paramattha dhamma, and there is no involvement in concepts. We have heard this before, but we have to hear it again and again before it sinks in. Our goal is the understanding of the reality appearing at this moment. We do not go any further than this moment. If we think of problems or situations there is no understanding of the reality appearing at this moment.

Through right understanding of nāma and rūpa we shall be more convinced of the truth of kamma and vipāka. This moment of seeing or hearing is result of kamma, a deed done in the past. We cannot know which kamma of the past produces result at a particular moment, but it is helpful to know that a pleasant or unpleasant result is conditioned by a deed we performed. Nobody can prevent the result from taking place. We cannot blame other people. When we, for example, are disturbed by the noise of a radio or the noise made by the neighbours' children, we can remember that hearing is vipāka and that thinking with aversion is akusala citta which arises at another moment. Then the object of citta is the present reality and we are not carried away by thinking of concepts. When confidence in the truth of kamma and vipāka arises there will be less fear and worry. Acharn Sujin said to Sarah and Jonothan:

"When you understand dhamma as dhamma, you see that everything occurs because of conditions. We fall asleep and get up again, because of conditions. When there are problems, it is because of conditions. There are just different realities, and even though realities appear, ignorance cannot understand them. We take realities for 'something' all the time. But awareness can 'flash in' any time, because of conditions, and that is the right awareness."

Acharn Sujin said that one actually lives alone and that it is most helpful to realize this. We have heard this before, but it becomes more meaningful when there is more understanding of the difference between the moment the object of citta is a paramattha dhamma and the moment we are thinking of a concept of a person or a thing. If we are disturbed by other people it seems that there are people, but what is the reality? Only a citta which thinks. When we are back to the present reality, the paramattha dhamma, we know that we are living alone, and such a moment is beneficial. In the ultimate sense, there are only nāma and rūpa, no people. When we are thinking, we live in our own world of thinking. No matter in the past, in this life or the next life, one always lives alone.

During the discussions Acharn Sujin stressed that we should see dhamma as dhamma. We may say that everything is dhamma, just a reality, but right understanding has to grow so that whatever reality appears now can be seen as just a dhamma, no person or thing, no self. We have to hear this again and again, but Sāriputta, when he heard a few sentences about realities, understood immediately and realized dhamma as dhamma. He had accumulated paññā for aeons.

We read in the "Vinaya" (Book of the Discipline, Part 4, Mahāvagga I, 23, 3-5) that Sāriputta asked Assaji what the doctrine was the Buddha had taught him. Assaji answered that he was not long gone forth and could therefore not teach Dhamma in full, but only briefly. Sāriputta asked him to explain the meaning of it, saying that he did not need a great elaboration. We read:

> "Then the venerable Assaji uttered this terse expression of dhamma to the wanderer Sāriputta:
>
> 'Those dhammas which proceed from a cause (hetu), of these the Truthfinder has told the cause.
>
> And that which is their stopping (nirodho)- the great recluse has such a doctrine.'
>
> When the wanderer Sāriputta had heard this terse expression of dhamma, there arose dhamma-vision,

> dustless, stainless, that 'Whatever is of the nature to
> uprise all that is of the nature to stop.' He said: 'If
> this is indeed dhamma, you have penetrated as far
> as the sorrowless path, unseen, neglected for many
> myriads of aeons.' "

Sāriputta understood directly the four noble Truths: dukkha, the cause of dukkha, its ceasing and the way leading to its ceasing. We have intellectual understanding of the four noble Truths, but when paññā has been developed to the level of satpaṭṭhāna they can be directly realized without having to think about them.

Seeing now arises because of conditions, it is part of the cycle of birth and death. Seeing has to fall away, and thus, it is dukkha. Sāriputta immediately understood that right understanding of the reality arising at the present moment leads to the elimination of ignorance and craving which are the conditions for being in the cycle of birth and death, the conditions for seeing, hearing and the other realities which arise. He understood the reality of the present moment as dhamma, arising because of conditions. He penetrated its characteristic of anattā.

For us it is difficult to see dhamma as dhamma because ignorance covers up the truth. We read in the commentary to the "Book of Analysis" (the "Vibhaṅga", the second book of the Abhidhamma), in the "Dispeller of Delusion" (Sammohavinodanī, I, Ch VI, Classification of the Structure of Conditions, 140) about ignorance which is opposed to understanding. We read:

> "That is to say, knowledge is understanding. It makes
> known and plain the four Truths with each meaning
> and each cause. But this ignorance when it arises
> does not allow that (understanding) to make that
> (dhamma) known and plain; thus, because of its op-
> position to knowledge, it is unknowing ..."

We then read that whenever ignorance arises it does not allow understanding to penetrate, to grasp and to rightly consider the truth. Thus, each time it arises it blocks and hinders the operation of understanding. This text reminds us of the activity of ignorance which is unnoticed, because when there is ignorance we do not know that there is ignorance. It is very treacherous.

We need to develop understanding of paramattha dhammas life after life, in order to see dhamma as dhamma, to see it as anattā. We cling to the idea of "our whole body", but when there is touching, hardness is the dhamma which appears. The idea of the whole body is only in one's memory. Acharn Sujin said:

"When there is touching, where is your head, where are your legs? Only in your memory. When there is touching you may not realize it as merely a moment of experiencing an object. Deep in your mind there is still the idea of 'something'. For instance, when you touch something in the dark you like to know what it is, thus there is still 'something'. There are only six doors, and one object is appearing at a time. It does not stay, waiting for you to touch it."

Several conditioning factors are needed for the experience of hardness, such as the rūpa which is hardness and the rūpa which is bodysense. Also these conditioning factors are themselves conditioned. Hardness and softness are characteristics of the Element of solidity, one of the four Great Elements and this is conditioned by the other three Elements of cohesion, heat and motion arising together with it. The rūpa which is bodysense is produced by kamma. The experience of tangible object through the bodysense is vipāka, the result of kamma. We see how intricate the combination of different conditioning factors are; they are just there for a moment of experiencing hardness. We cannot direct the coming together of these factors and none of them can last. They are only present for an extremely short while, they are insignificant dhammas.

Some people want to concentrate on rūpas of the body. By focussing on one point of the body they believe that they can notice the rūpa which is bodysense. The bodysense is all over the body but when tangible object impinges on the rūpa which is bodysense, it does so only on one point. That extremely small particle is then the rūpa which is the physical base for body-consciousness, and it is also the doorway through which tangible object is experienced. When a rūpa like heat or hardness is impinging on the bodysense it can hurt and painful feeling arises. But can we directly experience the rūpa which is the bodydoor, arising and falling away where there is impingement at that moment? It falls away immediately. It is useless to try to find out where the impingement was.

Acharn Sujin explained that one does not own anything:

"One thinks of one's whole body and of one's possessions as belonging to oneself, but there isn't anything one owns, not even visible object in this room. It arises, appears and falls away. The succession of different rūpas which are visible object conditions the concept of 'something'. We can see how fast citta arises and falls away, it can lure us like a magician. If we do not know this there is 'I' and 'mine' all the time. Does sound belong to anyone? If it is your voice, does it belong to you?

Visible object is just a rūpa out of twentyeight rūpas. It is the only reality that can be seen. We find our thoughts about visible object so important, but visible object is only a kind of rūpa. When one has understanding of visible object and of thinking, one sees the difference between the absolute truth and the conventional truth."

When we have more understanding of the difference between seeing and paying attention to shape and form, it will be clearer when the object of citta is just one reality, appearing through one of the six doors, and when the object is a concept. In the absolute sense there is no owner of anything, but does it then make sense to try to acquire possessions? There was a discussion about this topic in the house of our friends Ivan and Ell. Ivan used to think that when one contemplates Dhamma one should have fewness of wishes. Then there is no need to expand one's business in order to make more money. Now he understands that right understanding should be developed in a natural way, that one should not try to change one's life style. If one is a layman one should not try to live the monk's life, a life of contentment with little. Acharn said:

"We have lobha, no matter whether we work or do not work. We work because we were born. Working is only seeing, hearing, smelling, tasting, touching and thinking. You don't have to change yourself or prepare yourself for Dhamma, you don't have to devote all your time to it, but develop understanding of this very moment, in order to see it as just dhamma. Seeing and visible object are just dhammas, everything in one's life is dhamma. But one does not see dhamma, one does not understand dhamma as it is. One tries to spend time on dhamma, to change one's life, but just now there is dhamma."

People are wondering why they always have so much lobha. Acharn Sujin remarked:

"It is the function of lobha to cling, that is why there is clinging. We cannot change its characteristic or function. This reminds us that lobha is dhamma, it arises because of its own conditions, it is there as object of which right understanding can be developed."

The Buddha taught the monks, the nuns and the layfollowers, men and women, to develop satipaṭṭhāna, each in their own situation and each following their own life style, so that they would see dhamma as dhamma.

We read in the "Gradual Sayings" (Book of the Eights, Ch VII, § 10, Earthquakes) that the Buddha, while he was at Cāpāla Shrine, gave Ānanda three times the opportunity to ask him to live on for his full life-span. Ānanda did not ask him to do so, since his heart was possessed by Māra. After Ānanda had left, Māra came and said to the Buddha that he should now pass away. After his enlightenment the Buddha had said to Māra that he would not pass away until his disciples were able to practise the Dhamma and to proclaim it. Since this was now the case Māra asked him to pass away. The Buddha answered that he would pass away after three months. We read that he "cast away the sum of life" and that there was a great earthquake. In this sutta we are reminded of what is to be expected of the Buddha's followers.

We read further on in the same sutta that the Buddha, after his enlightenment, had said to Māra:

> "I shall not pass away, O Evil One, until my monks shall be disciples, learned, trained and courageous, who have attained peace from bondage, who are erudite, Dhamma-bearers, perfect in righteousness of Dhamma, perfect in the right practice, who live in accordance with Dhamma- till they have taken Dhamma as their teacher and can proclaim it, teach it and make it known, can establish it, open it, analyze it and make it plain to others- till they can confute any counter-teaching which has arisen, and which may well be confuted by Dhamma, and can set forth sublime Dhamma."

We read that the Buddha had said exactly the same about the nuns and the layfollowers, men and women. The commentary to this sutta, the "Manorathapūranī, explains "erudite", in Pāli: bahussutta, as having listened to the three Piṭakas (Parts of the teachings). The commentary then adds that one is bahussutta as to "pariyatti", the intellectual understanding, and as to "pativedha", the realization of the truth. One should be "Dhamma-bearer" in both ways. This reminds us that it is not enough to only listen and read. There should be the development of understanding of whatever reality appears up to the level of satipaṭṭhāna so that the truth can be directly experienced. The disciples should be perfect in righteousness of Dhamma. We read that the commentary states:"They practise the Way of vipassanā which is the Dhamma fitting to be ariyan Dhamma."

The Buddha's followers should take Dhamma as their teacher. Acharn Sujin reminded Sarah and Jonothan again that we should not be dependant on someone else. She said:

"Take Dhamma as your teacher, do not depend too much on others. The understanding of realities depends on your own consideration. I do not like to depend on others. It has to be my own struggle to understand the teachings. You do not need someone else to tell you how much understanding you have. This present object will tell you."

There is visible object now. We can check whether it is understood as just a dhamma or whether there is still "something" in it. Nobody else has to tell us. Dhamma is our teacher.

Appendix A

Pāli Glossary

akusala unwholesome, unskilful

anattā non self

anumodana thanksgiving, appreciation of someone else's kusala

arahat noble person who has attained the fourth and last stage of enlightenment

Buddha a fully enlightened person who has discovered the truth all by himself, without the aid of a teacher

citta consciousness the reality which knows or cognizes an object

dhamma reality, truth, the teaching

dukkha suffering, unsatisfactoriness of conditioned realities

jhāna absorption which can be attained through the development of calm

kamma intention or volition; deed motivated by volition

kasiṇa disk, used as an object for the development of calm

khandhas aggregates of conditioned realities classified as five groups: physical phenomena, feelings, perception or remembrance, activities or formations (cetasikas other than feeling or perception), consciousness.

kusala wholesome, skilful

lokuttara citta supramundane citta which experiences nibbāna

nāma mental phenomena,including those which are conditioned and also the unconditioned nāma which is nibbāna.

nibbāna unconditioned reality, the reality which does not arise and fall away. The destruction of lust, hatred and delusion. The deathless. The end of suffering

rūpa physical phenomena, realities which do not experience anything

samatha the development of calm

satipaṭṭhāna applicatioms of mindfulness. It can mean the cetasika sati which is aware of realities or the objects of mindfulness which are classified as four applications of mindfulness: Body, Feeling, Citta, Dhamma. Or it can mean the development of direct understanding of realities through awareness.

sīla morality in action or speech, virtue

Tathāgata literally "thus gone", epithet of the Buddha

Tipiṭaka the teachings of the Buddha

vipassanā wisdom which sees realities as they are

Appendix B

Books by by Nina van Gorkom

The Buddha's Path An Introduction to the doctrine of Theravada Buddhism for those who have no previous knowledge. The four noble Truths - suffering - the origin of suffering - the cessation of suffering -and the way leading to the end of suffering - are explained as realities that can be directly experienced in today's world.

Buddhism in Daily Life A general introduction to the main ideas of Theravada Buddhism.The purpose of this book is to help the reader gain insight into the Buddhist scriptures and the way in which the teachings can be used to benefit both ourselves and others in everyday life.

Abhidhamma in Daily Life is an exposition of absolute realities in detail. Abhidhamma means higher doctrine and the book's purpose is to encourage the right application of Buddhism in order to eradicate wrong view and eventually all defilements.

Cetasikas. Cetasika means 'belonging to the mind'. It is a mental factor which accompanies consciousness (citta) and experiences an object. There are 52 cetasikas. This book gives an outline of each of these 52 cetasikas and shows the relationship they have with each other.

The Buddhist Teaching on Physical Phenomena A general introduction to physical phenomena and the way they are related to each other and to mental phenomena. The purpose of this book is to show that the study of both mental phenomena and physical phenomena is indispensable for the development of the eightfold Path.

The Conditionality of Life This book is an introduction to the seventh book of the Abhidhamma, that deals with the conditionality of life. It explains the deep underlying motives for all actions through body, speech and mind and shows that these are dependent on conditions and cannot be controlled by a 'self'. This book is suitable for those who have already made a study of the Buddha's teachings.

Survey of Paramattha Dhammas A Survey of Paramattha Dhammas is a guide to the development of the Buddha's path of wisdom, covering all aspects of human life and human behaviour, good and bad. This study explains that right understanding is indispensable for mental development, the development of calm as well as the development of insight. Author Sujin Boriharnwanaket, translated by Nina van Gorkom.

The Perfections Leading to Enlightenment The Perfections is a study of the ten good qualities: generosity, morality, renunciation, wisdom, energy, patience, truthfulness, determination, loving-kindness, and equanimity. Author Sujin Boriharnwanaket, translated by Nina van Gorkom.

www.ingramcontent.com/pod-product-compliance
Lightning Source LLC
Chambersburg PA
CBHW020448100426
42813CB00026B/3000